*The Organization and Planning
of Adult Education*

The Organization and Planning
of Adult Education

Theodore J. Kowalski

STATE UNIVERSITY OF NEW YORK PRESS

Published by
State University of New York Press, Albany

© 1988 State University of New York

For information, address State University of New York
Press, State University Plaza, Albany, N.Y. 12246

Library of Congress Cataloging-in-Publication Data

Kowalski, Theodore J.
    The organization and planning of adult education / Theodore J.
Kowalski.
        p.   cm.
    Includes index.
    ISBN 0-88706-798-0.   ISBN 0-88076-799-9 (pbk.)
    1. Adult education—Administration. 2. Adult education—Planning.
I. Title.
LC5225.A34K68 1988
374-dc19   87-34014
                                                                     CIP

10   9   8   7   6   5   4   3   2   1

To my wife *Mary Anne*

Contents

Figures

Preface

Although demography is not a precise science, rather persuasive evidence exists to suggest that the only growth areas for educational programs in the next two decades will be adult and continuing education. Two developments support this forecast. First, there simply will be more adults in proportion to the remainder of the society in the future. Life expectancy is increasing, and the "baby boomers" soon will be beyond the child-bearing years. Second, the complexities of working life and personal needs are combining to lead more adults to abandon outmoded ideas about education being a youth-oriented activity. In essence, lifelong learning is a reality which is gradually being recognized.

Even today, adult education is narrowly defined by many citizens. It is perceived to be a compensatory program, providing basic skills (such as reading and writing) for those who never successfully completed high school. Indeed, much of what was labeled "adult education" in the first half of this century focused on basic adult education and vocational programs. Typically, the local public schools and, increasingly, community colleges were the providers of these services. This restricted view and arena of adult education are no longer valid. Today programming occurs not only in myriad subjects, but also in a variety of environments.

The narrow scope of adult education in the past restricted interest in the topic of program planning. Since the vast majority of offerings was in school settings, program development complied with the procedures used by the school systems or community colleges. But as adult education spread to private industry, trade unions, churches, libraries, the military, and countless other organizations, program planning emerged as a critical area of study. Graduate students in adult education now need to be prepared to assume leadership positions in institutions which possess varying cultures, resources, and attitudes toward adult education.

This book is devoted to examining the organizational context in which adult learning programs are offered. Organizational theory is infused throughout, offering the reader a foundation for understanding the relationship of the sponsoring agency and the dynamics of structured learning activities. Detailed studies of topics such as organizational climate, organizational development, and conflict resolution have not been common in adult education. In large measure, the absence of these issues in textbooks is explained by the historical patterns in the field which already have been mentioned. For the contemporary student who is preparing for a working life that may extend three or four decades into the future, the diversity in practice makes analysis of the organizational context an absolute necessity.

The basic elements of program planning constitute the second half of the book. Using the organizational context, the reader will find practical suggestions for proceeding with tasks such as needs assessment, advisory councils, and budgeting. The debilities of technical models are examined, and both linear and nonlinear paradigms are illustrated. The final two chapters of the book examine the effects of refinement in adult education and how the future is apt to alter even more the challenges and responsibilities of administrators who select this field of social service.

The underlying premise is that effective leaders are educated rather than trained: that is, administrative excellence stems from the ability to analyze, construct contingencies, and select appropriate courses of action. Training, by contrast, emphasizes prescribed responses to certain conditions. The educated leader has mastered knowledge related to the adult as learner, understands the potential relationships between the sponsoring agency and specific educational programs, and is capable of predicting the potential effects the environment will have on the entire process.

A good number of the students who enroll in a course in planning adult education programs will not have had exposure to the study of organizational theory. Likewise, the vast majority of practitioners already planning programs lack an understanding of this topic. For these audiences, this is an especially cogent book.

A special note of appreciation is extended to Donna Merrell for assisting with the editing; to Cheryl King for developing the graphics; and to Professors James McElhinney, Peter Murk, Roy Weaver, and George Wood, my colleagues in Teachers College, who offered their advice and expertise. Finally, appreciation is expressed to Professor John Fallon of Saginaw Valley State College, Saginaw, Michigan, for co-authoring Chapter 13.

Theodore J. Kowalski

PART I

Organizational Context

CHAPTER 1

The Organizational Aspect
of Adult Education

Bob and Mary have just completed doctoral programs in adult education. They are having lunch together before departing from the campus to the world of work. Bob has accepted a postion with a large urban school system as director of adult education. Mary will begin work for a manufacturing company specializing in home appliances. Her title is director of staff development. Both are excited about the challenges that lie ahead, and their luncheon conversation centers on the positions they soon will occupy and their educational experiences that prepared them for these positions. As they exchange information, both begin to understand just how different their work environments will be.

Bob will function in a public, service-oriented setting. What occurs in adult education in this organization is conditioned by a multitude of forces. Administrative style, political considerations, fiscal resources, educational priorities, and available facilities exemplify the factors which impact upon program planning and presentation in public school systems. Mary, by contrast, will work in private industry. The priorities, procedures for making decisions, and the nature of prevailing policies are likely to be different from those Bob will encounter. As they continue their discussion, Bob and Mary also analyze their graduate school experiences and the extent to which those experiences provide a springboard to the realities of being a practitioner. They consider the degree to which their shared formal education has prepared them to assume leadership responsibility in diverse organizational environments. In particular, they ponder the extent to which their academic studies prepared them to understand organizations and how they function.

This encounter serves to highlight one major challenge of adult education. Unlike specialized leadership programs in business and public administration, adult educators need to be prepared to work in a variety of organizations,

3

institutions, and agencies. Professors of adult education realize that they must
give their students a balance of instruction, amalgamating knowledge about
the adult learner with a variety of leadership studies. Currently, there is much
discussion among professors and practitioners concerning the desired content
of graduate studies.

On the one hand, there are contentions that the study of adult education
is deeply rooted in educational foundations (such as history of education or
philosophy of education). Accordingly, those who embrace this position believe
that the preparation of adult educators should remain the exclusive domain of
colleges of education (for example, Galbraith and Murk, 1986). Conversely,
there are those who advocate a broadening of preparation, especially into areas
of study commonly housed in departments of behavioral sciences or colleges of
business. The effects of the latter position were verified in a recent study of
doctoral programs in adult education in which slightly more than half of the
professors surveyed agreed that the field was moving toward human resources
development (Kowalski and Weaver, 1986). Regardless of philosophical inclinations, however, most graduate programs in adult education recognize the need
to prepare students to encounter the challenges of program development.

THE INSTITUTIONAL SETTING OF ADULT EDUCATION

As American society has been shifting from an industrial base to an
informational foundation, there has been an immense increase in the attention
given to the study of organizational leadership (Naisbitt, 1982). This is true in
large measure because organizations now exhibit tremendous variance in purpose, philosophy, composition, administrative structure, and even culture.
Unlike the first half of the century, when most were industrial, profit-seeking,
manufacturing entities, the contemporary organization is just as likely to be
nonprofit, human intensive, professionally dominated, and service oriented.
Mental health clinics, medical clinics, educational institutions, YMCAs and
YWCAs, and the like exemplify common service agencies exhibiting weighty
differences in operations from private businesses.

Adult education has become one of the fastest growing areas of human
services. Technology, leisure time, changing values, and changing job markets
are but a few of the stimuli fueling the surging demand for programs. This
expansion creates expected needs with regard to organizing, developing, and
managing adult learning experiences. This book concentrates upon the programming aspects of adult education. The diversity of settings in which these
programs occur, the relevance of organizational theory to the planning process,
and the principles of program planning are the primary areas of emphasis.

Program planning is essentially an administrative responsibility. It entails aspects of leadership (knowing what should be done) and management (knowing how to do it). Thus, the practitioner requires some level of specialized education relating to organizational behavior and program planning within the realm of adult education. This notion is clarified by examining the whole arena of administration as it relates to adult education.

ADULT EDUCATION ADMINISTRATION

Some question why it is advantageous to specifically study the administration of adult education. After all, do not principles of leadership and management lend themselves to all situations? Would it not be more efficient for adult educators to simply enroll in educational administration classes with those graduate students preparing to be school principals and superintendents? Or would it not be more judicious for prospective administrators of adult education to complete degrees in business administration? Many are inclined to answer in the affirmative to these questions. As a result, it is not uncommon for administrators of adult programs to have little or no academic background in working with nontraditional students; for example, they might have a background teaching industrial and vocational education at the high school level (Roudebush and Fallon, 1984). In private industry, personnel specialists frequently are selected to design learning activities even though many lack formal training to do so.

With this historical pattern, it is little wonder that some challenge the necessity of specialized administrative study within the realm of adult education. The proliferation of programs and the gravity of changes in society suggest, however, that practitioners must be exposed to higher levels of specialization than was true in the past. Contemporary administrators ought to be able to provide a linkage between the theoretical aspects of teaching adult learners and the theoretical aspects of program development and administration— and they must be prepared to do so under conditions which may vary significantly. Most importantly, they must be able to build bridges between knowledge they acquire in formal studies and the world of work.

On the typical university campus, administrative study is conducted in a variety of academic departments. The most common include educational administration, public administration, business administration, hospital administration, and hotel and restaurant management. Even departments such as sociology, psychology, and communication sciences are establishing a foothold in declaring scholarly domains for aspects of leadership study and organizational behavior. This diversification exists for three primary reasons. First, there is the belief that leaders must have a high level of technical knowledge related to the area being supervised. For adult education, this means understanding the psychology of the adult learner, teaching techniques with adults, and the like. Second, there is the belief that leadership study is most meaningful when it is applied directly to a specific field of practice. And finally, there is the belief that administration, per se, does not constitute a separate academic discipline, but rather involves the applications of knowledge to varying situations (Owens, 1981).

Although some aspects of leadership in adult education are not unique, others certainly are. This is true in large measure because of the diversity of settings in which adult education occurs; but it is also true because adults differ in many respects from children as students. So although the creation of budgets may entail the same skills required of managers in public schools or private industry, other responsibilities, such as program planning, necessitate specialized study. Gradually, the curricula of adult education have expanded, encompassing leadership courses and devoting more attention to human resources development. In most institutions, graduate study in adult education is a blend of courses focusing upon the teaching act, learning theory, behavioral sciences, and leadership.

A SPECIAL FOCUS

As noted previously, the focal points of this book are environmental diversity, the relevance of organizational theory, and elements of successful program planning. Each of these topics is invaluable to achieving the knowledge level required for effective program planning. Further, leadership is viewed as a situational activity—one largely dependent upon circumstances surrounding the practitioner. For this reason, leadership education is perceived as a process of preparing one to develop and use contingencies. This approach is most likely to produce practitioners capable of functioning effectively in diverse organizational settings. Unlike training programs that emphasize learning to cope with specific situations, education should provide critical thinking skills which are adaptable to all situations.

Every learning experience designed for adult clients is affected by a multitude of factors. For this reason, the administrator ought to be prepared to deal with contrasting values, including client aspirations of life-style, parent organization priorities, societal expectations, and personal beliefs (Knox, 1980). In recognition of these conditions, enlightened scholars are beginning to advocate that practitioners stop relying upon simple, linear models to plan programs. Rather, they are encouraged to explore more complex, integrated models which recognize that adult education does not occur in a value-free vacuum (Simpson, 1982). In fact, the reliance upon simple, technical models of planning has been a major deficiency in adult education programming (Brookfield, 1986).

Research is given special prominence in this book. The practitioner who understands and has the ability to apply research and theory to everyday decisions has several distinct advantages as a leader. First, the salient features of a situation become more apparent in the first stage (the diagnostic stage) of decision making because the practitioner associates real situations with a theoretical knowledge base. Second, the practitioner is more likely to include and combine crucial ingredients in the early stages of decision making. Again, associations to research data allow a more detailed investigation of contingencies and alternatives. Finally, the practitioner who uses research is more likely to appreciate the influential dynamics at the implementation stage of decisions (Knox, 1980). In the absence of such a knowledge base, the administrator usually is guided by personal judgments, chance, or imitations of practices in other organizations. These alternatives are risky.

A recent research study examining planning efforts in adult education revealed that the vast majority of models advocated for adult education lack theoretical foundation (Sork and Buskey, 1986). Rather than providing the underlying assumptions and theoretical propositions, many of the popular planning models are "how to do it" formulas more appropriate for training than for graduate education. A more sophisticated approach to program planning in adult education is one which addresses the dynamics of organizational climate and its many ramifications. Such programming is more cumbersome and necessitates sacrifices, especially with regard to efficiency and simplicity.

ORGANIZED VERSUS UNORGANIZED ADULT EDUCATION

Definitions of adult education can vary significantly. Knowles (1982), for example, provides three different definitions based upon orientation. In a general orientation, he includes all experiences by which new knowledge, understanding, skills, attitudes, interests, or values are acquired as adult education. In a technical orientation, he restricts the definition to organized activities conducted by a variety of institutions toward the achievement of specific educational objectives. And in a professional orientation, Knowles views adult education as a social practice which includes all individuals, institutions, and associations working toward the continued education of adults. These three definitions reflect the range of thinking as to what could be labeled "adult education."

Darkenwald and Merriam (1982) create a definition largely on the assumption that schools and colleges are agencies of socialization whose principal purpose is to prepare children and young people for adult life. Their definition reads as follows:

> Adult education is a process whereby persons whose major social roles are characteristic of adult status undertake systematic and sustained learning activities for the purpose of bringing about changes in knowledge, attitudes, values, or skills. (p. 9)

In this book, a division is made between those learning activities which are organized and those which are not. Self-directed learning is not disputed as a valid method of acquiring knowledge or skills; however, this portion of adult education is basically not discussed here. Congruent with the assumption of Darkenwald and Merriam, "regular" college and university academic programs also are not included as part of adult education. Although it could be argued that college students are indeed adults, only the continuing education and extension education aspects of colleges and universities are considered to be components of organized adult education.

The guiding definition used for adult education programs is as follows:

> the organized, deliberate, and purposeful design of learning activities for mature persons occurring in organizations but excluding the regular programs of traditional educational institutions.

Organized means that there is a systematic structure, rational order, and unity to the process. The design is deliberate in that there is thorough consideration and awareness of consequences, and it is purposeful in that a desired result is to be attained (Fallon, 1985). Traditional educational programs include the normal curricula of elementary schools, secondary schools, and colleges and universities. Special schools, for example, proprietary schools, are excluded from the category of traditional educational institutions. That adult education occurs within organizations is central to this definition.

THE RELATIONSHIP OF ADULT EDUCATION TO THE ORGANIZATION

Organized adult education does not occur in isolation: the process is planned and executed as a subsystem of a parent organization. This relationship is referred to as the "institutional aspect" of adult education. Since the institutional setting pervades the vast majority of adult programs, the application of organizational knowledge is a critical factor for the adult education administrator. The variety of parent organizations for adult education will be discussed in greater detail later in the book; however, it is important to note what has already been stressed—that the organizations which sponsor adult programming vary markedly in structure and purpose.

Four key factors interact when organized adult education occurs. They include the general environment in which the organization exists, the parent organization, the adult program, and the learners. The relationship among these four is illustrated in figure 1-1. The environment refers to the elements

Figure 1-1
INTERACTING FACTORS IN AN ADULT EDUCATION PROGRAM

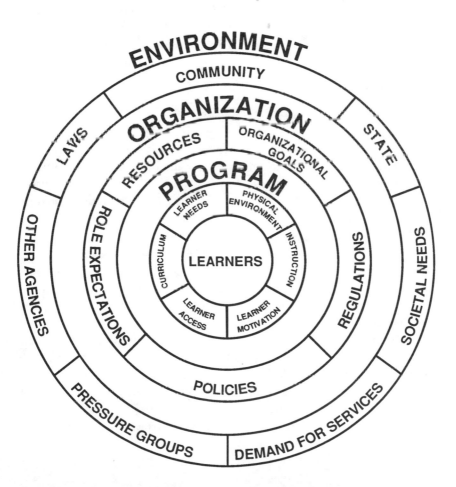

external to the parent organization. This would include the local community, the state, or even the nation in which the organization functions. The parent organization is the institution which chooses to engage in some form of organized learning program for adults. The program includes the specific nature of the offering (for example, a course in computer literacy). The learners are the clients who bring their own values and needs to the classroom. The reality surrounding this interaction illuminates the need for each occurrence of adult educaton to be addressed as a unique experience.

Any organization that attempts, in the long run, to employ a single organizational structure or procedure is apt to incur serious problems (Schmuck et al., 1977). This is true for the most part because the world and its societies (environment) are changing so rapidly. The organization, much like a person, adjusts to cope. Not surprisingly, adult education programs also will suffer if they choose to remain static. Since the environment is changing and since the organization is apt to be changing, inflexible approaches to program design will eventually become outdated and fail. For this very reason, a special emphasis is given to organizational theory as a prelude to discussing models and components of actual program planning. This discussion occurs in the second part of this book.

SUMMARY

Adult education is a growing enterprise in a changing world. The proliferation of adult programs has spawned the need for more persons to assume leadership roles in this field. Administrative study is typically conducted as a subpart of the specialization to which it is applied. This trend is holding true for adult education. As a result, graduate study (especially at the doctoral level) is expanding to include leadership courses.

Although adult education can be defined in many ways, this text views the process as an organized, deliberate, and purposeful activity. As such it does not include self-directed learning or educational experiences which occur in the regular offerings of elementary schools, secondary schools, colleges, and universities.

The effective use of research and existing knowledge by the practitioner is predicated upon the awareness of the interaction of the environment, the parent organization, the adult programs, and the learners. This interaction clarifies the contention that program development, as a critical aspect of administration, is a process which does not lend itself to single solutions. Rather, each program presents the practitioner with a novel challenge which necessitates an understanding of the adult as a learner, the environment as a restricting variable, and the parent organization as a controlling variable.

FOR FURTHER DISCUSSION

1. In what ways have the advancements of science and its application, technology, increased the demands for adult education?

2. What would be the problem(s) with employing persons with degrees in business administration to administer adult education programs?

3. What problems might an administrator encounter if he or she simply adopted a program format for an adult program that has been successful in another organization?

4. List several ways in which an environment could restrict the development of adult educaton programs.

5. List several ways in which the parent organization could control the nature of an adult program.

REFERENCES

Brookfield, S, (1986) *Understanding and facilitating adult learning.* San Francisco: Jossey-Bass.

Darkenwald, G., and Merriam, S. (1982). *Adult education: Foundations of practice.* New York: Harper and Row.

Fallon, J. (1985). *The concept of adult education.* Unpublished paper, Ball State University, Muncie, IN.

Galbraith, M. and Murk, P. (1986). Adult education should remain the exclusive domain of colleges of education. *Eastern Education Journal, 18,* 13-17.

Knowles, M. (1982). *The modern practice of adult education.* Chicago: Follett.

Knox, A. (1980). Approach. In A. Knox (Ed.), *Developing, administering, and evaluating adult education* (pp. 1-12). San Francisco: Jossey-Bass.

Kowalski, T., and Weaver, R. (1986). Graduate programs in adult education: An analysis of doctoral programs and professorial opinions. *Proceedings, 1986 midwest research-to-practice conference in adult, community, and continuing education* (pp. 79-84). Muncie, IN: Ball State University.

Naisbitt, J. (1982). *Megatrends*. New York: Warner Books.

Owens, R. (1981). *Organizational behavior in education*. Englewood Cliffs, NJ: Prentice-Hall.

Roudebush, D., and Fallon, J. (1984). A study of career patterns, professional mobility and job satisfaction levels among public school adult education administrators in Indiana. *Proceedings of the 25th annual adult education research conference* (pp. 178-183). Raleigh, NC: Department of Adult and Community Education, North Carolina State University.

Schmuck, R., Runkel, P., Arends, J., and Arends, R. (1977). *The second handbook of organizational development in schools*. Palo Alto, CA: Mayfield.

Simpson, E. (1982). Program development: A model. In C. Klevins (Ed.), *Materials and methods in adult and continuing education* (pp. 92-98). Los Angeles: Klevens Publishing.

Sork, T., and Buskey, J. (1986). A descriptive and evaluative analysis of program planning literature, 1950-1983. *Adult Education Quarterly, 36*(2), 86-96.

CHAPTER 2

Basic Considerations

To the average citizen, adult education remains a vague concept. Many are quick to identify the process as night classes for those persons who never were able to graduate from high school or shop classes for persons needing vocational training. Although both perceptions are correct, they represent a very small part of what is appropriately labeled "organized adult education."

Throughout this century, there has been a growing investment in organized education in America. The number of public and private schools rose rapidly as the value of education in a democratic society became more highly recognized. Periodically, there were concentrated efforts to guide this growth, either through philosophical positions or political influence. The reform movements of the 1950s and the 1960s, for example, reflected national reactions to stimuli such as Sputnik and the passage of civil rights legislation. These reform efforts typically concentrated on youth and, as such, fortified the notion that education was most meaningful if it occurred in the early years as a preparation for adulthood. In the past two decades, however, there has been a growing awareness that many adults also need and desire to engage in formal learning experiences. This increased consciousness stimulates a multiplicity of agencies to enter the adult education market in an attempt to satisfy the demand.

The purpose of adult education may focus upon the needs and desires of the learner, the needs and desires of the sponsoring organization, or the needs and desires of society. For example, the YMCA's reason for offering a course in computer literacy may be substantially different from American Motors's reason for offering the same program. Yet both activities are considered forms of adult education.

As mentioned, this book emphasizes the variables which tend to make each challenge of program development a novel leadership responsibility. This chapter explores three basic and foundational variables which are partially

13

responsible for creating this uniqueness. They include the adult learner, the history of adult education in America, and the identification of major issues which have changed the scope and magnitude of adult education. For some readers, these topics may cover material with which they are already familiar. For the novice to adult education, they provide a brief overview of several relevant factors.

DEFINING THE ADULT LEARNER

Who is the adult learner? Are determinations between adults and nonadults essential to educational programming? These and similar questions are fundamental issues confronting the organization and the administrator. One primary cause for the ambiguity that continues to surround adult education is the lack of understanding of what adulthood really means. Further, there are the questions which center upon the potential differences between adult and preadult learners. In other words, to what extent should adult education be different from the process of educating children? Defining the adult learner requires that both sets of questions be addressed.

The Adult

Persons frequently use the phrase *act like an adult*. There are activities in society which are restricted by laws or social standards to "adults only." There are even "adult theaters" which often are patronized by persons who behave more like juvenile delinquents rather than mature human beings. The term *adult* is used in so many different contexts that confusion is an expected outcome. To complicate matters further, attempted definitions of adulthood range in length, complexity, and specificity.

The most common method of defining adulthood is chronological age (Kimmel, 1980). This is true in large part because of local, state, and national laws. The use of age in law provides a convenient method for coping with policies which must have general application to the population. Age is quantifiable; thus, it is a classification which is easy to understand and administer. Yet age alone provides a most restrictive definition. Age does not address maturity, socialization, or similar attributes which may be observable but difficult to quantify.

When persons are expected to act in an adult manner, the criterion of cultural expectation is usually being expressed: that is, certain behaviors are expected from individuals who have reached this level of maturity. Karp and Yoels (1982) describe this cultural expectation as the way people feel about themselves socially. Thus, adulthood may mean the manifestations of self-expectations which reflect behaviors which society deems as mature. The person who is socially mature may be treated as an adult even though chronologically he is in his teens.

To some, adulthood is determined by physiological or biological criteria. Since everyone develops at a slightly different pace, some high school students may look more like adults than do some twenty-five-year olds. It is commonly recognized, nevertheless, that looks can be deceiving. Physical appearances may be incongruent with emotional development, mental development, and self-discipline. A person may appear to be twenty-two but manifest the behavior of an adolescent.

Another criterion for categorizing adults is social roles. For example, a person who is married may be considered an adult regardless of age, social maturation, and so forth. A person who quits school at age sixteen and goes to work in a factory may be considered an adult in certain social circles. In fact, many students who drop out of school before high school graduation see this act as accelerating their quest to reach adult status. Not going to school may increase the likelihood of their being allowed to exhibit behaviors which previously were restricted (for example, being allowed to smoke at home).

Finally, there are very complex descriptions of adulthood. One example of such a complex system is offered by Karp and Yoels (1982) in their life cycle perspective of adulthood. Here a linear method is used to categorize persons into various life stages. Since it is assumed that all human beings pass through these stages, adulthood is a product of one's stage in life. Another complex system of classification has been developed by Havighurst (1972). Here development tasks are divided into stages, and adulthood is dependent upon achieving a certain level of development within the classification system. These tasks are the products of cultural expectations, physical development, individual values, goals, and social readiness.

In this book, adulthood will be viewed in an eclectic manner: that is, no one criterion will be used to determine adult status. The onset of adulthood normally will occur in the late teens to the early twenties. Social roles, individual maturity, occupational requirements, and the like are other criteria which appropriately are considered. For example, an eighteen-year-old person who is married, socially mature, and required to become computer literate to maintain his or her position as a shipping clerk would be considered a candidate for adult education. On the other hand, a twenty-one-year-old college senior who simply is going to school full time because he or she doesn't know what else to do may not be considered a student of adult education. In general, this book identifies adults as those who have the potential for engaging in formal learning activities beyond the scope of traditional education (secondary school, undergraduate education).

The Adult Learner

A second prerequisite to a detailed study of the organization and the development of adult programs is the analysis of the adult learner. Specifically, differences between adult learners and others are extremely relevant to administrative tasks. If administrators believe that adults learn and behave differently than do traditional students, this belief obviously affects critical program decisions. Likewise, if an administrator believes that all adults have the same needs, values, and learning styles, this belief, too, would condition programmatic directions.

Knowledge about the adult learner emanates from the writing of experts, from everyday experiences, and from the findings of research. The opinion that teaching adults is a unique arena of the education profession meriting specialized training is based largely upon a theoretical model called "andragogy."

Both the word and the model of andragogy were popularized by Malcolm Knowles (1982). In a quest to establish a process separate from pedagogy (the teaching of children), he formulated primary assumptions about adults as students:

— Their self-concept moves from one of being a dependent personality toward a self-directed human being.

They accumulate a growing reservoir of experience that becomes an increasingly rich source of learning.

Their readiness to learn becomes oriented increasingly to the developmental tasks of their social roles.

Their time perspective changes from one of postponed application of knowledge to immediacy of application, and accordingly, their orientation toward learning shifts from one of subject centeredness to one of performance centeredness. (Knowles, 1982, pp. 44-45)

In essence, andragogy suggests a teacher role which is more responsive and less directive. The model encourages high levels of self-directed learning with the adult student having input regarding content, methodology, learning assessment techniques, and even program design.

Andragogy has been widely accepted among adult educators in America. Many believe the concept to be the very justification of adult education as a separate field of study. In recent years, however, skepticism has been voiced.

Most notably, the implicit assumption that pedagogy specifies a single methodology correct for all learners (the assumption that provides the very foundation of andragogy) has been questioned. Contrary to some interpretations, pedagogy does not connote a single methodology for teachers, but simply refers to the general practice of teaching children. Critics have noted that the pedagogy/andragogy division would be more appropriately addressed by using the terms *teacher-directed* and *self-directed* rather than by focusing upon the teaching of children versus the teaching of adults (Rachal, 1983). Other concerns about the universal application of andragogy as a model for adult programming have been voiced by Courtenay and Stevenson (1983), Knudson (1980), and Lebel (1978). The issue of andragogy is central to program planning. Its wide acceptance fosters the use of general practices in adult educaton. Most notably, the belief that adults should be highly involved in program planning may radically reduce the contingencies considered in program planning by the administrator.

The notion that andragogy has been responsible for some inflexibility in program planning deserves considerable attention. By concentrating on the learner, the planner is more prone to reduce the importance of the learning task and learning environment. The tasks of learning to read and learning to decorate a cake typically are not of equal importance in our society. Likewise, the tolerance for planning methods may vary significantly from one organization to the next. Believing that all adult learners are, in large measure, a homogeneous group makes the use of simplistic planning models more likely.

Relevance of subject matter is a key variable for success in all learning situations, and it is especially crucial for adults. Greater independence prompts adults to withdraw more readily from impertinent experiences. This aspect of andragogy appears valid. Adults frequently are alienated by educational programs that do not adequately address their personal needs (Mezirow, 1981). Nevertheless, the high demand for relevance is not a mandate for universal self-directed learning. Subject matter relevance may be exceedingly high in a variety of instructional modes, even those dominated by teacher direction.

In reviewing research concerning differences between adult learners and children, Kowalski (1984) found that the following appear to be factors where differences exist:

- Motivation (adults are more motivated)
- Physical speed (adults lose speed as they age)
- Personality (adults exhibit more fixed behaviors)
- Vision and hearing (these factors are regressive)

- Independence (adults are more independent)

- Expectations (adults demand high levels of relevance)

Areas where differences were not found include the following:

- Intellectual capacity

- Performance on intelligence tests (provided appropriate tests are used)

- Individual adaptations to instructional modes (adults, like children, exhibit different success rates with varying instructional modes)

In sumary, adult learners do exhibit some notable differences from children. These differences, however, should not be exaggerated. Adult learners are individuals who differ from one another. The need to recognize individual learner needs is especially crucial when the process of program development is being considered. The temptation to generalize principles to all adult learners, and consequently to all adult programs, has been great. The most obvious manifestations of this temptation have been (1) the assumption that all adult education ought to be organized as a learner-directed experience, and (2) that institutional, linear models are the one best way to plan programs. The issue is not whether learner-centered methods should be applied universally by teachers of adults, but whether teachers should be capable of choosing appropriate methodology to suit the students and situation (Beder and Darkenwald, 1982). Likewise, it is myopic to believe that one model of program planning is best for all situations. These conclusions are central to the theme of this book: that program development is a process which is based upon the uniqueness of a given situation. Thus, developing a program for General Motors may be substantially different from developing a program for a community college, not only in organizational environment but in clientele as well.

ADULT EDUCATION IN THE PAST

Historically, the United States has trailed some western European countries in the development of adult education programming. In fact, many practices used in this country have their origins in Great Britain. Over the past three decades, there has been a proliferation of opportunities and requirements resulting in more adults becoming engaged in formal learning activities. This growing demand has been the central force igniting expansion.

Initially, adult education was viewed as a compensatory activity. It provided basic skills to those who did not acquire them in elementary school programs (reading, mathematics). Gradually, it also focused upon vocational or trade training, attempting to provide job skills for those who had difficulty acquiring employment. These early areas of emphasis circuitously contributed to the abuses of trying to teach adults as if they were children. This practice was due in large measure to the use of elementary and secondary school teachers in adult education programs.

Before the twentieth century, there were several notable efforts for adult education in America. The lyceum was the earliest. This process attempted to bring a community together for lectures and discussions. As an organized function it recognized the needs and interests of adults. In a similar fashion, the Chautauqua Institute in New York created an even more organized learning center where adults could pursue education. On another front, colleges and universities were expanding both in numbers and complexity in the 1800s. In the later part of that century, university extension and correspondence teaching became outgrowths of this expansion and additional facets of adult education in America (Ulrich, 1965).

Adult education grew most rapidly in large cities where there were concentrated populations of adults and immigrants. The agency which most often provided this service was the public school system. It seemed logical that the school system which was already engaged in the teaching and learning process could offer adult education at the most reasonable cost. And especially during the first two decades of this century, efficiency was deemed critical. Urban school systems were caught up in the frenzy of technical and economic efficiency, a conspicuous product of the industrial revolution (Callahan, 1962). Adult classes were organized and offered at night, usually using the same facilities, physical resources, and human resources which were used to teach children during the day. Needless to say, many adult students did not adapt well to these conditions.

Gradually, other organizations started to engage in various forms of adult education. Libraries, the military, and even private corporations adapted various forms of organized instruction which could be labeled as "adult education." The early attempts at providing these programs faced many barriers. Inadequate financing, a lack of understanding about adult learners, and a prevailing attitude that education was a function of childhood were among the most severe. It is important to realize that adult education in America stemmed largely from basic and vocational needs. Accordingly, the programs were far less diversified than would be true today.

The history of adult education is substantially more complex than is portrayed here. Its basic growth pattern from urban school districts to colleges and universities and ultimately to a wide range of organizations in society is

important. Understanding this pattern helps to explicate the prevailing
methodologies and beliefs which dominate modern practice.

THE CURRENT FOCI OF ADULT EDUCATION

Contemporary adult education today bears little resemblance to the efforts
posted sixty and seventy years ago. Although basic education and vocational
education remain essential elements, the field has expanded to the point where
virtually all types of institutions and agencies find themselves engaging in components of the teaching and learning act. Divisions of adult education have
been established within most state departments of education. Funding for adult
programming has increased markedly. Private industry is changing rapidly with
regard to recognizing individual worker needs as well as organizational needs.
But the greatest change has been the acceptance of the concept of lifelong
learning: that is, the American public is abandoning the notion that organized
education is solely for children. This modified attitude has had a significant
impact upon the quality and quantity of adult education. The acceptance of
lifelong education is merely the gradual recognition of an empirical reality.
Adults, by choice or necessity, continue to learn throughout the developmental
stages of life (Brookfield, 1983).

A second factor which has affected the direction and scope of adult education is the rapid development of technology. The introduction of the microcom-
puter into the workplace, for example, has created needs for even the best-
educated adults. Given the fact that the rate of technological development is
accelerating, the effects of science upon everyday life are going to become even
more pronounced in the future. This scenario illuminates the importance of
lifelong learning to society and the individual.

The third issue is the growing amount of leisure time. Technology is
partially responsible for earlier retirements, shorter workweeks, and the like.
These alterations spawn a multitude of societal and personal needs and problems. Increased leisure time generates needs with regard to recreational
education, instruction related to hobbies, and even formal academic study (such
as learning a foreign language). Abundant leisure time also can generate
problems related to mental and physical health.

One other factor worth mentioning relates to the tendency of adults to
change careers. Unlike fifty years ago, many Americans do not feel locked into
their jobs. Rather, the tendency of adults to contemplate a change in jobs, even
including radical alterations in occupations, is on the rise. Stories of forty-year-
old medical students or corporate executives becoming artists are not as rare
as they once were.

The tasks for the contemporary planner are indeed entangled. Confusion about the nature of adult learners, incertitude about teaching methods, and the heterogeneity of sponsoring organizations have raised practitioner awareness of the difficulties related to program planning. This enlightenment, unfortunately, has had little impact in moving planners away from using simplistic models or from relying upon "common sense."

SUMMARY

The task of program development needs to be preceded by a basic understanding of the terms *adult* and *adult learner*. Although there are many ways to define an adult, an eclectic approach which considers a myriad of factors results in the most accurate description. Under these circumstances, the onset of adulthood may begin in the late teens.

Much of the current practice of adult education is based upon the perception that adults differ markedly from children as learners. Although this is essentially true, the perception has led many to conclude that all successful adult learning needs to be highly student centered. This notion has been challenged in recent years. Increasingly, scholars are viewing adult education as a situational task; the design of each program is dependent upon the students, the available resources, the goals, and the sponsoring organization. In other words, programs ought to be developed with an awareness of the context in which they will occur.

Finally, the foci of adult education have expanded significantly from the early part of the twentieth century. The awareness that learning is lifelong, the advances of technology, the increases in leisure time, and the increasing tendency for adults to change occupations exemplify why adult education has become more complex.

FOR FURTHER DISCUSSION

1. Why would classification of adults according to chronological age present problems for some adult education programs?

2. List several reasons why all adult education should or should not be learner directed.

3. What effect(s) did immigration to the United States have upon the early years of adult education?

4. List several reasons why you believe funding for adult education never has been equal to funding for the public education of preadults.

5. How has increased leisure time affected the demand for adult education programs?

6. Why wouldn't techniques proven to be successful in secondary school programming be equally effective in the design of programs for adults?

REFERENCES

Beder, H. W., and Darkenwald, G. C. (1982). Differences between teaching adults and pre-adults: Some propositions and findings. *Adult Education, 32,* 142-155.

Brookfield, S. (1983). *Learners, adult education, and the community.* Milton, Keynes, England: Open University Press.

Callahan, R. E. (1962). *Education and the cult of efficieny.* Chicago: University of Chicago Press.

Courtenay, B., and Stevenson, R. (1983). Avoiding the threat of gogymania. *Lifelong Learning: The Adult Years, 6*(7), 10-11.

Havighurst, R. J. (1972). *Developmental tasks in education.* New York: McKay.

Karp, D. A., and Yoels, W. C. (1982). *Experiencing the life cycles: A social psychology of aging.* Springfield, IL: Charles E. Thomas.

Kimmel, D. C. (1980). *Adulthood and aging.* New York: John Wiley.

Knowles, M. S. (1982). *The modern practice of adult education.* Chicago: Follett.

Knudson, R. S. (1980). An alternative approach to the andragogy/pedagogy issue. *Lifelong Learning: The Adult Years, 3*(8), 8-10.

Kowalski, T. J. (1984). Research and assumptions in adult education: Implications for teacher preparation. *Journal of Teacher Education, 35*(3), 8-11.

Lebel, J. (1978). Beyond andragogy to gerogogy. *Lifelong Learning: The Adult Years, 1*(9), 16-18.

Mezirow, J. (1981). Critical theory in adult learning and education. *Adult Education, 32,*3-24.

Rachal, J. (1983). The andragogy/pedagogy debate: Another voice in the fray. *Lifelong Learning: The Adult Years, 6*(9), 14-15.

Ulich, M. E. (1965). *Patterns of adult education.* New York: Pageant Press.

CHAPTER 3

A Typology for Parent Organizations

The study of program planning in adult education necessitates an analysis of the organizations that sponsor such activities. This is true because the institutional context assumes a major role in shaping the behaviors of the programmer and other administrators responsible for formulating key decisions. Unfortunately, the tremendous diversity among the sponsoring organizations constitutes a barrier to comprehensive study. In order to overcome this obstacle, some method needs to be devised to simplify the process.

One practical approach to reducing complexity is the creation of a classification system: that is, some method is devised to allow organizations to be grouped according to characteristics cogent to the practice of adult education. This process results in a typology—a mechanism which allows more detailed study by reducing the range of differences among the institutions being studied.

The typology formulated and used in this book does not include adult education provided by a single individual. Rather, the emphasis is upon institutionally supported programs. It is possible for a single person to deliver educational services in a planned, purposeful manner to others (such as by tutoring); however, this type of educational program does not entail the dynamics which are the foci of this book. Moreover, individual providers constitute a very small percentage of the total activity in adult education in America (Knowles, 1982). Similarly, adult education which is conducted individually without the intervention of a second party (self-teaching) is excluded from consideration. Rather, the planning and delivery of adult education services within the context of an organization are the nuclei of the typology developed here. This portion of adult education, which constitutes the vast majority of programming occurring in the United States, is what is referred to as "institutionally based adult education" (Darkenwald and Merriam, 1982).

23

EXISTING CLASSIFICATION SYSTEMS

A number of typologies have been formulated for the specific purpose of analyzing parent organizations engaged in adult education. Each provides some novel approaches to classification. Three of them will be presented here. Their selection was based primarily on their contrasting features; as such, they exemplify the diversity of existing typologies. Probably the least known and used of these was created by Graham Mee and Harold Wiltshire (1978). These British authors presented their work in the book *Structure and Performance in Adult Education.* Their typology is based upon the use of seven dimensions. The position of an organization with regard to each of these dimensions reveals differences among organizations. The seven dimensions used are the following:

- Formal link (the extent to which the organization formulates formal associations with other agencies)

- Staffing (the degree to which full- or part-time employees are used)

- Environment (demographic, economic, educational)

- Size (number of courses, number of students)

- Teaching accommodation (own, hired, borrowed)

- Management (degree of autonomy, democratic decisions)

- Philosophy (dominant concept or purpose)

The authors also identify five primary types of adult education institutions:

- Specialized institutions

- Colleges of further education (continuing education)

- Community schools and colleges

- Adult plus youth institutions

- Leisure institutions

This typology is somewhat complicated, and its application to American institutions is not widely used. Nevertheless, the framework serves to exemplify one manner in which classification is achieved. Each of the five types of institutions can be broken down according to the seven characteristics. This process could create thirty-five separate categories of adult education organizations.

The second effort considered here is the typology developed by Wayne Schroeder (1970). His work first appeared in the *Handbook of Adult Education.*

A more detailed typology was presented in the book *Building an Effective Adult Education Enterprise* (1980). Schroeder's work is quite comprehensive but also a bit complicated. He categorizes controlling organizations by program types. The outline below illustrates the structure of his work:

I. Agent systems

    A. Leadership systems

        1. State, regional, and national governments
        2. Professional associations of adult education
        3. Private foundations
        4. Graduate programs of adult education

    B. Operating systems

        1. Institutional agencies

            a. Autonomous adult education agencies
            b. Youth education agencies
            c. Community service agencies
            d. Special interest agencies

        2. Voluntary associations

            a. Pressure groups
            b. Community betterment groups and service clubs
            c. Mutual benefit societies and social clubs
            d. Professional associations

        3. Individual agents

            a. The entrepreneur
            b. The volunteer

II. Client systems

    A. Membership client systems

        1. Internal agent membership systems
        2. External agent membership systems

    B. Nonmembership client systems

        1. Geographic criteria
        2. Demographic criteria
        3. Social role criteria
        4. Interest criteria
        5. Individual and social need systems

III. Eclectic systems

As previously mentioned, this typology is comprehensive but difficult to use. It is an effective system for providing specificity for certain analysis; however,

for studying the relationship of the parent organization and the planning of
adult education programs, it is a bit too detailed. Reading the full text of
Schroeder's work is nevertheless highly recommended for those students and
practitioners of adult education who intend to specialize in organizational
planning.

The third typology developed by Darkenwald and Merriam (1982) is the
least complex of the three. This framework attempts to place all agencies
providing adult education into four primary categories. The outline for the
framework is listed below:

I. Independent adult education organization

   A. Community-based agencies (such as nonprofit adult education
centers)

   B. Proprietary schools

   C. External degree agencies

II. Educational institutions

   A. Public schools (elementary/secondary)

   B. Community colleges

   C. Four-year colleges and universities

   D. Cooperative extension services

III. Quasi-educational organizations

   A. Cultural organizations (such as the public library)

   B. Community organizations (such as the Rotary Club, the League of
Women Voters)

   C. Occupational associations (such as the American Medical Association)

IV. Noneducational organizations

   A. Business and industry

   B. Government agencies

   C. Armed forces

   D. Unions

   E. Correctional institutions

   F. Other (includes a range of agencies such as hospitals, mental health
clinics)

Although this effort to provide a meaningful division of agencies is the easiest to comprehend, it is perhaps too general. First, the number of categories, four, results in many divergent organizations being placed in the fourth category, *noneducational organizations*. Placing correctional institutions in the same category with General Motors, for example, produces a restricted level of analysis for program planning purposes. Second, some of the emerging agencies in the adult education arena are relegated to a subcategory of the fourth category, *noneducational institutions—other*. Since hospitals and mental health clinics are increasing their adult education efforts, they should receive more focused attention. Placing them in an *other* category does not give adequate attention to their importance in comtemporary adult education.

AN ALTERNATIVE TYPOLOGY

Using Schroeder's work (1980) as a foundation, a new typology was formulated for this book. This typology uses six categories for identifying sponsoring organizations. As previously mentioned, the primary purpose of using a typology is to provide a framework which illustrates how organizations differ in purpose, functions, climate, and other relevant factors. The reader is reminded that it is the application of a typology in the context of program planning that is integral to this book. The six categories of the new typology include the following:

Type A: Institutions which provide adult education as an exclusive function

Type B: Educational institutions which offer adult education as a secondary function

Type C: Community service agencies which provide adult education as a secondary function

Type D: Private organizations and agencies which provide adult education as a secondary function

Type E: Voluntary organizations and groups which provide adult education as a secondary function

Type F: Government agencies which provide adult education as a secondary function

TYPE A. There are institutions that exist solely to provide adult education services. The four most common are proprietary schools, institutions which have the sole purpose of offering external degrees to adults, residential adult centers, and nonresidential adult centers. Also included in the Type A category would be certain consulting firms. Type A institutions with regard to control are classified as private/profit, private/nonprofit, or public. Proprietary schools are, of course, all privately owned and managed. The vast majority are profit-seeking organizations. External degree agencies also are included here, provided their sole function relates to providing programs for adults. Correspondence schools are declining in popularity as many accredited institutions of higher education are entering this market through their continuing education programs.

TYPE B. A variety of educational institutions engage in adult education either as a secondary function or as a corollary to their primary mission(s). Public school districts are one of the most common providers of adult services in this category. Because public schools are already delivering educational services, because their facilities are not occupied seven days a week and twenty-four hours a day, and because the public schools are locally controlled (in all states except Hawaii), they are viewed as an ideal agent to offer extended services to adults. The formality of structure with regard to adult education may vary extensively in school districts. In large, urban systems, an entire division of the administrative structure may be created to serve the needs of adult education. In smaller districts, the entire program may consist of several adult classes with no specialized regular teachers or administrators.

Community colleges (formerly referred to as "junior colleges" in many parts of the country) are another Type B provider of adult education. In fact, in many community colleges, adult education has become a very important part of operations. Although some would argue that adult education is not a secondary mission for community colleges, the primary mission of the vast majority of these schools remains the education of students who have just completed high school. The local control aspect of many community colleges and the presence of expensive laboratories and equipment provide conditions most conducive to adult education. In addition, many adults prefer to attend classes at a community college instead of a night class at the local high school. No doubt, social factors and self-esteem contribute to this preference. In many instances, attendance at community colleges also results in greater extrinsic rewards (for example, an employer is more apt to reward college level work).

Regular (four -year) colleges and universities also provide adult education as a secondary function. Many of these institutions now have separate divisions for continuing and extension education. The acceptance of adult education at colleges and universities historically has been less than at community colleges, in part because of a greater acceptance of the nontraditional student (and flexibility to meet this student's unique needs) in the community college environment. But changes in philosophy and the realities of demographics (in many parts of the country colleges are competing for a smaller pool of students) are prompting four-year institutions to roll out the welcome mat to nontraditional students.

One additional type of institution worth noting in Type B are independent professional schools. There are hundreds of law schools, medical schools, and similar professional colleges (pharmacy, optometry) which are not a part of a comprehensive college or university. These institutions are commonly referred to as "professional colleges." Most of the schools of osteopathic medicine, for example, fall into this classification, because only a small number of them are subsystems of comprehensive universities. Independent professional schools engage in adult education as part of a continuing education commitment to practitioners. As an illustration, the school may offer periodic workshops for practitioners to improve their skills. These workshops are a corollary to their regular curricula of preservice professional education.

TYPE C: In the past twenty-five years there has been a rather dramatic increase in the amount of adult education that occurs with community service agencies. These agencies are usually publicly supported. But some are private, and they may even be profit motivated. One commonality of the agencies in this category is the provision of services other than adult education as the primary service. Adult education is an outgrowth of the prime service(s) of the agency. Museums and libraries engage in adult education generally for the purpose of enhancing community life. Occasionally programs are offered which address specific needs of learners (for example, writing workshops). Hospitals and mental health clinics engage in adult education in a variety of ways. Typically, the nature of their adult classes relates to mental or physical health. Thus, classes in prenatal care and weight control may be common for a hospital, and a mental health clinic may be offering courses in conflict resolution, substance abuse, or stress management.

Other organizations in this category are the media. Public television, radio stations, and even newspapers may provide forms of adult education. In recent years, institutions of higher education have collaborated with public television stations to offer a variety of credit courses. The continuing technological advances in the media suggest that adult education through advanced forms of media will be a growing enterprise. Although public television is clearly a Type C agency, privately owned newspapers might be more appropriately placed in the next category, Type D.

TYPE D: Type D organizations are privately owned enterprises which offer forms of adult education as a corollary to their primary purpose for existence. Privately owned manufacturing companies would fall into this category. Frequently these companies engage in adult education not because of individual learner needs, but rather because of the needs of the organization. For example, a manufacturer of refrigerators may conduct classes for repairmen because their efficiency and capabilities in product maintenance are related to sales. Two issues are especially responsible for the proliferation of adult education in these organizations. First, technology is expanding so rapidly that education has become a necessity for a company to keep its employees current. Second, American industry is changing its values regarding services which are rendered to meet employee needs. Specifically, more companies are willing to invest in learning programs for their employees which may not be associated directly to the profit functions of the company. The improved employee morale and personal growth stemming from adult education may produce important benefits for the company in a circuitous fashion. This is a practice which has received more attention as a result of invidious comparisons with Japanese manufacturers.

Many private foundations also fall into the Type D category. Those that do are agencies which choose to engage in adult education to advance organizational values or philosophy. For example, a national organization against abortion might offer workshops in an attempt to persuade adults to accept its position. Even when foundations provide educational programs not specifically designed to advance their own positions, and even if adult education is not the primary purpose of the foundations, they should be classified as Type D.

TYPE E. Voluntary organizations and groups are playing a more important role in adult education. Included in Type E are entities that offer adult education as something other than their primary function—for example, labor unions. The union does not exist to provide education, but may do so to enhance its primary purposes or to simply provide services of interest to individual members. Some might argue that unions are not always voluntary; but given Right to Work laws in many states, they are essentially organizations where members exercise free choice in affiliation. Professional organizations, such as the American Bar Association or the American Medical Association, would also qualify as Type E organizations.

A variety of community groups are voluntary in nature and periodically engage in adult education. Service clubs (such as the Rotary Club or Exchange Club), social clubs (country clubs or similar ventures), and even pressure groups (county taxpayers association) are Type E. Also included are churches. Increasingly, churches are offering a range of programs for adults. These programs may be highly diversified, some having a direct religious purpose and others being directed to social or recreational purposes.

Perhaps the most prominent providers of adult education in this category are YMCAs and YWCAs. These organizations are committed to providing a range of recreational and educational services. They fall into this category and not Type A because education is not their exclusive or primary mission. In most instances, recreational activities are more dominant.

TYPE F. The final group of institutions involved in adult education are governmental agencies. One of the most prominent of these is the military. Increasingly, the military has forcused upon adult programming as a means of organizational improvement. Every branch of the armed forces now offers a variety of programs ranging from technical courses to basic education courses in very advanced tactical studies. The Community College of the Air Force exemplifies the manner in which adult education is becoming a major priority with the armed services. This operation offers programs for members of the Air Force throughout the world.

Various other local, state, and federal agencies provide forms of adult education. The United States Department of Agriculture makes available a number of educational programs for farmers and farm-related businesses. State agencies, such as the state board of health, offer workshops and classes to meet varied individual and societal needs. Even local governmental agencies, such as the police department, may offer courses for adult citizens. One of the fastest growing arenas of adult education is occurring in correctional institutions. The realization that education is a critical factor to rehabilitation is causing state and federal correctional departments to infuse educational programs into their operations.

ADDITIONAL CONSIDERATIONS

One value of a typology is that it exhibits the tremendous variety in the organizations which become involved with adult education. The classifications provide a framework that attempts to reduce the range of diversity so that analysis becomes less cumbersome. No doubt there are institutions that may not fit neatly into any one given category. There is also the realization that collaborative efforts are becoming more common. As the demand for services continues to grow and as resources become more limited, cooperative ventures among organizations are becoming an operational necessity. Thus an adult education program may be the product of the biases, needs, beliefs, and values of several different types of organizations.

There are other factors which could be used to classify parent organizations. Table 3-1 illustrates some of the more cogent ones.

Table 3-1

Classification Variables for Studying Parent Organizations

CLASSIFICATION VARIABLE	CLASSIFICATION OPTIONS
Ownership	Private Public Volunteer
Motive	Profit Nonprofit
Program purpose	Needs of society Needs of the individual Needs of the parent company
Organization purpose	Producing goods Providing services

The information in table 3-1 illustrates other possible variables for classifying organizations. An exhaustive listing of such variables would be extremely difficult. The dilemma facing the adult educator is selecting a typology which is neither too simplistic nor too complex. The six-category system presented here is designed to be a functional approach to separating organizations for purposes of further and more detailed study. Later in this book (chapter 6), this typology will be used to discuss the relevance of organizational theory to decisions in planning adult education programs.

SUMMARY

The use of a typology of parent organizations facilitates the study of organizational behavior and program planning. This is true because the identification of similarities allows a more conceptual approach to applying program-planning procedures in varying environments. A number of typologies have been formulated for use in adult education, and three were presented in this chapter. Some are quite cumbersome and others tend to be too basic.

A six-category typology was created and presented in this chapter to allow for the further study of organizations. This typology will be used later in the book as the application of theory and actual program planning are discussed. Excluded from the typology are programs developed by individuals rather than organizatons, agencies, or groups.

Many variables could be used to build a typology. The selection of specific factors is predicated upon the intended usage of the framework. In this instance, program planning was the dominant consideration.

FOR FURTHER DISCUSSION

1. Discuss how profit motives could affect an organization's decision to offer adult education classes. Also, discuss how profit motives might provide commonality in purpose with regard to adult education.

2. There are several types of organizations that do nothing but engage in adult education. List several with which you are familiar.

3. Review Schroeder's classification system in detail and point out its strong points and weaknesses.

4. Under what conditions might a privately owned newspaper be classified as a Type D organization?

5. Discuss the ways a typology would be used to identify adult education resources in a given community.

6. Try to identify any organization engaged in adult education which does not fit into one of the six categories of the typology presented in this book.

References

Darkenwald, G. G., and Merriam, S. B. (1982). *Adult education: Foundations of practice.* New York: Harper and Row.

Knowles, M. C. (1982). *The modern practice of adult education.* Chicago: Follett.

Mee, G., and Wiltshire, H. (1978). *Structure and performance in adult education.* London: Longman.

Schroeder, W. L. (1970). Adult education defined and described. In R. M. Smith, G. F. Aker, and J. R. Kidd (Eds.), *Handbook of adult education* (pp. 25–43).New York: Macmillan.

_____. (1980). Typology of adult learning systems. In J. M. Peters and Associates (Eds.), *Building an effective adult education enterprise* (pp. 41–77). San Francisco: Jossey-Bass.

PART II

Organizational Theory

CHAPTER 4

Understanding the Value of Research and Theory

The proliferation of organized educational programs for adults has spawned inquiry into efficacious methods for creating and administering adult learning experiences. To some extent, this inquiry is hampered by the sparsity of existing scholarly works devoted to this topic. Although much attention has been given to examining the nature of the adult learner (that is, the aspects of psychology and learning theory), far less literature and research have been devoted to the organization and development of programs. There is also a growing need to integrate research and theory with the knowledge and experience practitioners acquire through the workplace.

For the practitioner of adult education, problems associated with program development are exacerbated by the reality that planning can best be completed using sophisticated models which address numerous human and environmental issues. These factors are contextual variables deserving consideration in planning (Brookfield, 1986). History suggests that much of the failures and successes in the early stages of adult education programming were products of trial and error. Decisions were frequently made on the basis of common sense, innuendo, and chance. These impetuous approaches to planning have led scholars to recognize the value of infusing organizational theory and program development into the existing components of graduate studies in adult education. If programs are to be properly organized and managed, the existing knowledge of organizational behavior and dynamics needs to be made available to students and practitioners. Knowing students but not the organization can create an imbalance in decisions.

The study of organizational behavior requires exposure to several related topics. This chapter explores these topics and provides a foundation for more direct inquiry into how organizational behavior affects program development in adult education.

DEFINING THEORY

One common expectation of leadership is that persons in administrative roles will make decisions. Often the ability to achieve this expectation separates successful from unsuccessful administrators. Often we hear the criticism "He's a nice guy, but he won't make a decision." Avoiding decisions can create serious problems; but making a decision, per se, does not assure managerial success. Making the right decisions at least a reasonable percentage of the time is also a facet of meeting leadership role expectations. In fact, it is not a fear of decisions that plagues most leaders, but a fear of making the wrong decision.

Administrators of adult education face the same options that are encountered by all other types of managers. When confronted with circumstances demanding a decision, the administrator may choose from the following options:

- Ignore the situation and refuse to make a decison

- Make a decision on the basis of instinct (a "gut-level" reaction)

- Get someone else to make the decision for you

- Imitate the perceived successful decisions of another practitioner

- Make a decision on the basis of accumulated information which creates the likelihood that the response you choose will be effective

Any of the first four approaches may provide short-term relief, but continual reliance upon these options eventually creates problems. The final option, reacting on the basis of accumulated knowledge, indicates the behavior of an "educated" person. This approach entails the use of information to create alternative decisions, the weighing of these alternatives, and the selection of the one most suitable for the existing conditions.

Information used for decision making may be acquired in several ways. Personal experiences, observations, and systematic study are common paths to information. As knowledge is accumulated, associations can be drawn from the bits of information. These associations can be categorized and, as they accumulate, can provide a knowledge base for decisions. When one practices this technique in a scientific manner (in some ordered, purposeful manner), one is using the basic elements of theory.

What is the value of this systematic approach? Is decision making really a science, or is it an art? The administrator who can predict the likelihood of the success of alternative decisions is in a better position to make the most effective decision. This is especially true when the knowledge base is imposed upon the uniqueness of the variables under which the decision is to be made. Thus, the adult educator who understands how organizations function and who possesses a reasonable knowledge of organizational theory is more likely to be successful, particularly in the tasks of organizing and developing programs, if he or she uses this knowledge to make decisions.

What Theory is Not

The most common problem plaguing the use of theory is a lack of understanding of its essence. Misconceptions, particularly by practitioners, attenuate the potentialities of theory as a leadership technique. For this reason, defining theory appropriately commences with a review of three common misconceptions.

First, theory is not some sort of dream or idea representing the wishes of any one individual (or group). Likewise, theory is not a supposition or speculation. Finally, it is not a philosophical position expressing values which indicate the way things ought to be (Owens, 1981). Recognizing these misperceptions is extremely important. Administrators are quite prone to ignore theory. It is not difficult to understand why accepting theory as a dream, a supposition, or a philosophical view would diminish its utility to administrators who must deal with real problems every day. Ironically, this perversion mistakenly categorizes theory as a liability rather than an asset for leadership. These erroneous perceptions result in many practitioners viewing theory as impractical (Griffiths, 1964).

The Essence of Theory

The prevailing ambiguity related to theory is partially the result of variance in existing definitions. The absence of a universal definition has prompted many authors to write their own perceptions of theory. One frequently cited perception was written by Kerlinger (1973), and it describes theory as

> a set of interrelated constructs (concepts), definitions, and propositions that presents a systematic view of phenomena by specifying relations among variables, with the purpose of explaining and predicting phenomena. (p. 9)

Another definition primarily designed for applying theory to the study of educational administration was formulated by Hoy and Miskel (1982):

> Theory is a set of interrelated concepts, assumptions, and generalizations that systematically describes and explains regularities in behavior in educational organizations. (p. 20)

Finally, theory may be described in rather simple terms:

> A theory is a set of systematically related propositions specifying causal relationships among variables " (Black and Champion, 1976, p. 56)

This definition will suffice as a guide in this book.

Theories are used to synthesize, organize, and classify facts which emerge from observations and data collections in varying situations (such as research). Thus, they are developed by interfacing data collected on the same variables as they exist in varying environments. In summary, a theory is a frame of reference for categorizing facts. As such it becomes a meaningful approach to making decisions and solving problems (Combs and Snygg, 1970).

The illustration below identifies the hierarchy of approaches to decision making.

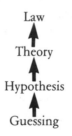

Law

↑

Theory

↑

Hypothesis

↑

Guessing

A law (or natural law) is a principle which has been verified beyond doubt and which provides knowledge about cause and effect that is used to govern behavior. A theory involves some degree of conjecture which provides probability of cause-and-effect relationships. A hypothesis is a provisional conjecture of cause and effect (or other relationships) which is to be tested. Guessing merely entails the use of intuition without integrating knowledge. Within this hierarchy, theory is the bridge between hypothesis (research) and natural law.

The Relationship of Theory and Research

The purpose of research is to generate knowledge which can be used as a basis for understanding phenomena and ultimately to aid in decision making (Wolpert, 1981). A research project typically involves the testing of a single hypothesis; however, it may involve the testing of multiple hypotheses. The following is an example of a hypothesis: Defining role expectations produces more effective work performance from nurses in a private hospital environment. The results of a single test of this hypothesis will provide valuable information;

however, the results of a single study have limitations which make generalizations to other environments and to other occupations quite risky. The reliance upon studies not replicated in diverse environments has been an especially troublesome issue for adult education.

When a series of research findings is categorized in a systemic fashion, theory building begins to take place. Using the example cited for nurses and role expectations, assume that identical studies were conducted with nurses in several other hospitals and for several other occupational categories in different environments (school administrators, salesmen, etc.). If the vast majority of the findings produced identical (or nearly identical) validating results, then one could develop the theory "that defining role expectations leads to more effective work performance." In this fashion, multiple research studies become the vehicle for building theory.

Research also may be used to test the validity of existing theories. Each time a researcher applies a hypothesis of defining role expectations to work behavior (assuming that the example used has been established as a theory), he or she will either fortify or weaken this theory. Thus, the linkage of research to theory may exist either as a process of theory building or as a process of theory verification.

THE USES OF THEORY

As mentioned previously, theory is a frame of reference for categorizing facts. But how does this frame provide a workable tool for the practitioner? How can theory be used in planning and the decisions related to planning?

Owens (1981) indicates that theory offers an accurate representation of reality, even if only a small slice of reality, by doing the following:

- Helping to organize our knowledge into a systematic, orderly body of knowledge
- Providing a guide for research
- Serving as a base for predicting consequences of actions
- Helping to explain phenomena that otherwise might be incomprehensible

This perspective of reality allows decisions to be made in a calculated manner. In the absence of such knowledge and systemic thinking, the primary attribute for leadership might simply be good old common sense.

A total understanding of human and organizational behavior entails more than the observable. Factors which are not always directly observable (for example, an individual's homeostatic state) also play a role in determining behavior. Theory allows for the interconnections among items of existing knowledge which often are available only in a scattered, fragmentary form (Parsons and Shils, 1951). In doing so, theory is a tool for the addition of information which in a sense is obscure. If all input data were infallible and readily known, theory would not be important. Obviously, this is not the case. Thus, theory helps the administrator to be more effective in the analyses of past actions and in planning the future by incorporating the known with the likely. By using the empirical data that are available, the administrator becomes more enlightened; consequently, decisions are approached with a pattern of conceptual rather than technical skills.

Miller (1958) states that with the use of theory in administration, the individual becomes efficient. Theory provides the administrator with a rational view of a situation which serves as a guide in the selection of principles. Leadership without theory is possible; however, the administrator usually is restricted to accepting the practices of others or chance. Emulating the deportment of others provides no guarantee that a given administrative decision will have equal effectiveness in different environments. Furthermore, the absence of theory does not permit the person to learn sequentially and systematically from experience. Rather than classifying experiences and drawing associations, the administrator muddles along depending upon trial and error.

This perspective on using theory provides a major justification of academic study in specialized fields. For the adult education administrator, graduate study should provide a format for understanding theories related to the adult learner, to curricula, to instructional techniques, to management, and to the organization and development of programs. Experiences in graduate education expose the student to theoretical science, the ultimate level of science. The student, through theoretical science, explores relationships and phenomena discovered in empirical science which help to explain underlying cause-and-effect relationships (Mouly, 1970).

ORGANIZATION AND THEORY

Earlier in this book adult education was defined as an organized, meaningful process. This definition omits self-directed learning, an omission which might offend some professors and practitioners of adult education. Nevertheless, this text focuses only upon those programs which are organized and, as such, programs which appropriately are viewed in the organizational context.

Organizations are complex and ambiguous entities. Too often, people do not see them in this manner. Theories can make a difference in determining whether a given situation is confusing or clear, meaningful or cryptic, a disaster or a learning experience (Bolman and Deal, 1984).

In our society, the term *organization* may assume many different meanings. Some authors (for example, Houle, 1972) engage in such specificity that they create esoteric distinctions between institutions and organizations, concepts often used synonymously in management literature. Here, however, the term *organization* is used in a simple yet formal manner to mean a link between structures. As such, an organization is defined as an integrated system of independent structures known as groups, and each of these groups consists of individuals (Berrien, 1976). An organizational plan is perceived as a means of achieving specified goals of an institution.

Organizational theory involves the systematic ordering of knowledge within the context of organizational behavior. This process includes the study of interaction among a particular organizational structure, individuals, groups, and the general environment. In the next chapter, three major organizational theories are discussed in detail. This material is designed to expand the use of organizational theory in developing adult education programs. Studying multiple perspectives is especially important. Too often, leaders become wed to a single view of how institutions function. Under this condition, a full understanding of behavior is virtually impossible (Bolman and Deal, 1984).

In adult education, the organizational format for programming should reflect the values, needs, and priorities of the sponsoring institution: that is, adult education (as a subpart of the organization) should be congruent with its organizational environment. Unfortunately, some institutions design instructional programs that ignore these attributes of the parent organization. When this occurs, the probability of programmatic problems increases. The association of adult programming to the sponsoring organization ought to consider the following three aspects of the educational programs:

1. The degree to which structure facilitates the achievement of desired ends (goals)

2. The degree to which structure reflects institutional values (philosophy)

3. The effects of structure upon individuals (teachers, adult learners)

Frequently, organizations are tempted to duplicate programs already in existence in other institutions. No doubt this approach to program development is quick and inexpensive, but it is also precarious. If serious problems occur with programs because organizational values, needs, and priorities were ignored, the dollars saved through inept planning will be outweighed by the costs incurred in attempting to correct the maladies once the programs are operational. Again, adult education practice has been plagued by the failure to use planning models and the reliance upon simplistic models.

There are several key concepts related to organizational theory which merit separate consideration. These include organizational climate, organizational development, organizational variance, and organizational adaptability.

Organizational Climate

Organizational climate refers to the elements which exist within the internal environment of an enterprise. These elements include policies, management styles, compensation methods, communication techniques, decision-making processes, and so forth (Kowalski, 1982). The climate may be expressed as understandings and expectations held in common by a majority of individuals within the organization. This common acceptance leads to expected uniformities in leadership and subordinate behaviors (Frederiksen, Jensen, and Beeton, 1972).

Climate usually is discussed in terms of a continuum of "open" to "closed." Open and closed organizations are discussed in greater detail in the next chapter; however, one should realize at this point that organizations are rarely, if ever, totally open or totally closed. Rather, they exhibit inclinations to being more open or more closed. Openness is an attribute which describes the degree to which an organization freely interacts with its environment. Most scholars, for example, contend that all public enterprises ought to be, by their very nature, open organizations (that is, they must interact to some degree with the populace who support and are served by their operations). Most private, profit-seeking companies, by contrast, tend to be closed climates.

Organizational Development

Organizational development, commonly referred to as "OD," has two primary functions. First, it is a conceptual framework of how organizations function. Thus, it involves the use of organizational theory. Second, it is a strategy that helps an enterprise to become self-correcting and self-renewing (Schmuck et al., 1977). In other words, organizational development is a procedure for understanding how organizations function and a method for allowing desired (directed) change to occur.

In adult education organizational development is a leadership responsibility that allows administrators to ensure that form (the structure of the organization) remains a product of function (the purposes of providing an adult program). Organizational development is the adaptive process of applying theory to real-life situations to allow planned changed to occur. Since the needs of persons served by adult education are not static, organizational development is a particularly cogent management concept.

Organizational Variance

As with people, not all organizations are alike. Although they share some commonalities (such as group interactions), organizations exhibit dimensions that establish them as unique entities. The most common dimensions of organizational variance are *geography, size, structure, leadership style,* and *goal direction.* The environment in which the institution exists is a critical geographic variable (for example, the services of an agency may vary substantially depending upon whether it is in a rural or urban environment). Size obviously refers to the number of individuals in the enterprise, and structure implies the line and staff relationships. Leadership style may be expressed as authoritarian, democratic, facilitating, and so forth; goal direction refers to the purposes of the institution (a private industry might offer adult education to improve the functions of the company, whereas the community library offers adult programs to enhance the quality of community life).

Understanding organizational variance is important because these identified differences provide a linkage to understanding behavior within the organization. Research studies, for example, have explored the causal relationships between certain organizational elements and innovation (Darkenwald, 1977; Baldridge and Burnham, 1975). These studies reveal how variables, in isolation or in combination, can significantly affect the behavior and outcomes of an organization.

Organizational Adaptability

Change occurs in different ways. Within organizations, the climate and other variables assume a large role not only in determining the process for change but also the nature of change. Change may be imposed by the environment (for example, a school district may add a computer literacy class for adults because thousands of signatures by patrons intimidate the school board to do so), or it may be a result of constructive adaptation (for example, a class in computer literacy may be added because periodic needs assessment conducted by the administration reveals its relevancy).

The adaptable organization is continually and consciously addressing demands initiated in the environment (such as the needs of adults in the community) and within the organization itself (such as new goals, new priorities) (Schmuck et al., 1977). Simply stated, adaptation is a process of changing to remain relevant. For obvious reasons, the adaptive organization exhibits high levels of environmental interaction.

The dynamic nature of adult education dictates that adaptability be a primary consideration and high priority for any agency providing such services. Changes in society and the rapid development of technology result in a diverse range of needs which must be addressed through adult education. Formal studies and informal observations indicate that institutions exhibiting higher levels of adaptability tend to be more likely to achieve their specified goals. Adaptability is the ultimate goal. It is the leadership activity of applying organizational theory, in light of unique variables and climate, through a systemic process of organizational development to meet ever-changing needs of adult learners.

THEORY AND CRAFT KNOWLEDGE

In large measure, the low esteem accorded theory by practitioners is a product of not understanding the real meaning and value of theory. It also is a product of what Brookfield (1986) terms the "theory-practice disjunction." Practitioners become dismayed with textbook approaches which simply fail to produce effective results in the real world. There is little doubt that earnest attempts to apply "academic approaches" have failed. But far too little is known about the failures to conclude that any one factor is responsible. Inappropriate application, misinterpretations, and the selection of inflexible planning models are common barriers to using theory effectively.

Far too many adult educators assume that the dichotomy between theory and practice is irresolvable. Therefore, one must choose; and since survival in the real world is important, the preference for successful work behavior mastered by other practitioners is prevalent. The accumulation of knowledge through practice is valuable, especially if this knowledge is systematically and categorically accumulated. It provides what is known as "craft knowledge."

Rather than perpetuating the gap between theory and craft knowledge, practitioners should direct their efforts to exploring connections for these two primary sources of leadership information. Moreover, craft knowledge is a greater asset if it is the product of analytical study. In this respect, it is formulated almost like theory. Just as it is risky to take a single research study and to generalize the results to all populations and settings, it is venturous to observe the behaviors of one or two administrators and to conclude that their successes can be adapted to all situations. Thus, the issues are (1) separating established craft knowledge from casual observation, and (2) linking theory and craft knowledge in practice.

Bolman and Deal (1984) point out that theories provide two valuable pieces of information. First, they tell the administrator what is important in a given situation and what can be ignored. Second, theories group different pieces of information into concepts. In a difficult process such as program planning, which occurs in varying organizational contexts, these two attributes of theory become critical to successful practice.

SUMMARY

This chapter explored the essence of theory. In doing so, nonexamples and definitions were presented. The linkage between research and theory also was discussed. The uses of theory by practitioners of administration have direct benefits for the quality of decision-making activities. The perception that theory is an abstract dream or philosophy has resulted in an out-of-hand rejection by many leaders, thus depriving them of one of their most effective tools for leadership.

Organizational theory, the systematic ordering of knowledge related to institutional behavior, is an especially cogent area of study for adult education administrators. Because programs may be developed in such a variety of institutions and environments, organizational climate, organizational development, organizational variance, and organizational adaptability are concepts which should be studied in relation to program design and development.

Far too many practitioners view theory as unrelated to the real world of work. They prefer to rely upon proven practices. Unfortunately, confusion exists between casual observations and genuine craft knowledge. The latter is a product of systematic classification; in this respect, it is quite similar to theory. Furthermore, the practitioner should not choose between theory and craft knowledge. Rather, the challenge is to link the two.

FOR FURTHER DISCUSSION

1. Discuss why administration in adult education could benefit from the application of theory.

2. Develop a sequence of hypotheses to be tested which can relate to a single theory.

3. Create a method (such as a questionnaire) to assess the level of understanding of the meaning of theory among leaders in a given organization.

4. Some critics might argue that the literature related to organizational theory is based primarily upon private industry experience and so has little or no relevance for adult education. Do you agree or disagree?

5. Describe how organizational variables may affect generalizations made about a single research study.

6. Discuss the differences between natural law and theory. Which is more powerful for predicting outcomes?

7. Discuss why organizations differ in the ability to adapt to change.

8. How does craft knowledge come into existence? Differentiate craft knowledge from theory.

REFERENCES

Baldridge, J. V., and Burnham, R. A. (1975). Organizational innovation: Individual, organizational, and environmental impacts. *Administrative Science Quarterly 20,* 165–176.

Berrien, F. K. (1976). A general systems approach to organizations. In M. Dunnette (Ed.), *Handbook of industrial and organizational psychology* (pp. 41–62). Chicago: Rand McNally.

Black, J. A., and Champion, D. J. (1976). *Methods and issues in social research.* New York: John Wiley.

Bolman, L., and Deal, T. (1984). *Modern approaches to understanding and managing organizations.* San Francisco: Jossey-Bass.

Brookfield, S. (1986). *Understanding and facilitating adult learning.* San Francisco: Jossey-Bass.

Combs, A. W., and Snygg, D. (1970). The challenge of psychology. In L. A. Negzer, G. G. Eye, A. Graef, R. D. Krey, and J. F. Overman (Eds.), *Interdisciplinary foundations of supervision* (pp. 2–7). Boston: Allyn and Bacon.

Darkenwald, G. G. (1977). Innovation in adult education. *Adult Education, 27,* 156–172.

Frederiksen, N., Jensen, O., and Beeton, A. A. (1972). *Predictions of organizational behavior.* New York: Pergamon Press.

Griffiths, D. E. (Ed.). (1964). *Behavioral science and educational administration.* Chicago: University of Chicago Press.

Houle, C. O. (1972). *The design of education.* San Francisco: Jossey-Bass.

Hoy, W. K., and Miskel, C. G. (1982). *Educational administration.* New York: Random House.

Kerlinger, F. N. (1973). *Foundations of behavioral research.* New York: Holt, Rinehart, and Winston.

Kowalski, T. J. (1982). Organizational climate, conflict, and collective bargaining. *Contemporary Education, 54,* 27–31.

Miller, V. (1958). The practical art of using theory. *The School Executive, 77,* 60–63.

Mouly, G. (1970). *The science of educational research.* New York: Van Nostrand Reinhold.

Owens, R. F. (1981). *Organizational behavior in education.* Englewood Clifs, NJ: Prentice-Hall

Parsons, T., and Shils, E. A. (1951). *Toward a general theory of action.* New York: Harper and Row.

Schmuck, R. A., Runkel, P. J., Arends, J. H., and Arends, R. I. (1977).*The second handbook of organizational development in schools.* Palo Alto, CA: Mayfield Publishing Company.

Wolpert, E. M. (1981). *Understanding research in education.* Dubuque, IA: Kendall/Hunt Publishing Company.

CHAPTER 5

Relevance of Organizational Theory

Organizational study is not a new scientific pursuit. Psychologists, sociologists, and other social scientists long ago recognized the importance of studying human behavior in the context of the organized system. In fact, some scholars conclude that the science of human behavior begins with organization (Malinowski, 1960).

This chapter reviews three organizational theories that are especially relevant to program planning in adult education. These options reveal the potential impact of organizational, group, and individual needs, goals, and behaviors. They also provide an evolutionary description of organizational theory.

Leadership studies have focused upon organizational theory with increased efficacy in the past two decades. Education professors realize that the basic components of this area of scholarly inquiry are applicable to a variety of settings. For example, teachers and nurses working in different environments react similarly to organizational dysfunctions (Carver and Sergiovanni, 1969). The investigation by social scientists of organizational dynamics provides important data for students and practitioners of educational leadership, including adult education.

As mentioned earlier in this book, organized adult education programs are those which go beyond incidental, personal learning experiences. Szczypkowski (1980) points out that adult education programs and practitioners are concerned with learning experiences which are deliberate, systematic, and sustained. These attributes provide the framework which illuminates the importance of the organizational context to this facet of educational programming.

Organizations are not static entities. That is not to say that organizations always move in intended directions. Although change is ubiquitous, the study of organizations reveals that action which produces change may be predicated by any number of factors. March (1984) identifies six:

1. Action resulting from the application of standard operating procedures and rules

2. Action related to problem solving

3. Action stemming from past learning

4. Action resulting from conflict

5. Action based upon diffusion (an action which spreads from one organization to another)

6. Action stemming from the needs, values, abilities, etc., of the organizational members

The adaptive behavior of organizations may or may not be visibly related to goals and objectives. Neither does unlimited change produce success. To understand organizations, one must study them in a similar way that a psychologist studies human and animal behavior.

Regardless of the sponsoring institution, adult education leaders benefit from understanding, and being capable of interacting with, the organizational environment in which they find themselves. In this regard, practitioners in private agencies, hospitals, public schools, colleges, and so forth have an equal interest in mastering the use of organizational theory as a tool for addressing the responsibilities of program development. In recent years, some researchers in adult education have started to explore ways in which practitioners are affected by their organizational setting as well as their clients (for example, Yeshewalul and Griffith, 1984).

The preceding chapter presented the criteria associated with organizational theory. This chapter explores primary theories, namely, the bureaucracy, the sociopolitical organization, and the open organization. The process of putting theory into practice is also reviewed.

THE BUREAUCRATIC ORGANIZATION

In our society, the term *bureaucracy* has for many become synonymous with waste and inefficiency. Some citizens, for example, view the government and its many agencies as expensive and unresponsive "bureaucratic boondoggles." Educational agencies have not been immune to these perceptions. But are all bureaucracies really inefficient? Does the average citizen actually understand the elements of a bureaucracy?

There is little doubt that bureaucratic theory frequently has been misunderstood and misemployed. Most public service agencies exhibit aspects of the bureaucracy, but there is some question as to whether these behaviors result from a percipient management decision (that is, the leadership in the organization understands and promotes a closed environment). A proper beginning to this topic is a brief review of the historical development of this theory.

The Origins of Bureaucracy

When Frederick Taylor wrote the *Principles of Scientific Management,* circa 1911, a new era of management theory was born. Taylor sought to develop the "one best way" to complete all industrial jobs. The focus of Taylor's research was efficiency of the individual worker in performing a particular task in the setting of the industrial shop. By using time and motion studies, human behavior and technical aspects of highly successful procedures were identified.

At approximately the same time in history a French industrialist, Henri Fayol, was studying administration in a broader (organizational) context. Fayol defined administration as planning, organizing, commanding, coordinating, and controlling (Robbins, 1976). He presented a format for acknowledging the multitude of components requiring coordination within an organization. His work exceeded the analysis of individual work tasks, and Fayol made some effort to apply his studies to nonindustrial settings.

A third contributor of bureaucratic theory, commonly referred to as "classical theory," was Max Weber, a German sociologist. Weber believed that authority was essential for ensuring proper organizational control, and that organizational control was necessary to achieve desired organizational goals efficiently (Weber, 1947). His work included the allocation of authority and responsibility within an organization. March and Simon (1958) identified four major interests of Weber as follows:

1. To identify the characteristics of bureaucracy

2. To describe its growth and reasons for growth

3. To isolate the concomitant social changes

4. To discover the consequences of bureaucratic organization for the achievement of bureaucratic goals (p. 36)

Weber's work was inspired by his desire to have the organization function rationally in a complex society.

The fact that these pioneers completed much of their work during, and immediately following, the Industrial Revolution is not coincidental. During this era, the less complicated methods of leadership were found to be lacking as new and sophisticated technology emerged and individual workers moved from isolated to social work environments. The three scholars mentioned here believed that a rigid structure of organizational control would promote rational, efficient, and disciplined behavior (Hanson, 1979). This structure would, in their view, offer the most effective means of achieving the established goals of any organization by reaching high levels of technical efficiency.

In *His Theory of Social and Economic Organizations,* Weber (1947) identified the following basic principles of a bureaucratic organization:

A hierarchical structure. An organization is developed in a pyramid type of structure; each administrator has responsibility for subordinates.

A division of labor. Workers and managers specialize in certain tasks and their work is restricted to these tasks. It is not necessary for a worker to know anything about the organization not directly related to his or her tasks.

Control by rules. Written policies direct the decisions of the organization. This practice ensures uniformity, predictability, and stability in management.

Impersonal relationships. Efficiency will be more readily realized if administrators use strict and systematic discipline over workers.

Career orientation. Administrators and workers are employed on the basis of developed expertise. Promotion results primarily from seniority. Salary is tied to rank in the organization.

A bureaucratic organization is designed to achieve technical efficiency by instituting an operational structure which is rigid and closed. The organization assumes a closed posture when it fails to recognize and interact with the external environment in which it exists (Katz and Kahn, 1966). At the time when classical theory was being developed, researchers were preoccupied with the "closed" perspective of organizations: that is, exploration was directed toward procedures which were designed to free the oganization from the burdens of external interventions.

The Use of Bureaucratic Theory in Public Organizations

As the work of the classical theorists began to gain wide acceptance in industry, the demands to adopt similar closed structures for public service organizations soon followed. Historically, the greatest pressures were placed upon school systems. This was not surprising in light of the fact that captains of industry often served on school boards in major metropolitan areas (Callahan, 1962). The large city districts pioneered practices which other school systems eventually emulated. When big city districts started to departmentalize and centralize power, for example, the smaller systems were often quick to model these experimental practices.

The inducement for schools to adopt the bureaucratic structure was quite similar to that for industry, namely, efficiency. The production line techniques of the industrial shop were myopically adapted to the classroom. This effort to maximize production in education (learning) at minimal cost ignored the uniqueness of a human-intensive, professionally dominated organization. Yet, despite the vast differences between the school and the factory, most school systems evolved, to a greater or lesser degree, as bureaucratic entities (Harper, 1965).

The implementation of rigid structure has many observable effects upon managerial delineation. The operation of a central office in a bureaucratic school district, for instance, would be identified by a clear demarcation of authority and responsibility. Only certain high-level managers (such as associate superintendents) would have direct access to the superintendent. Principals would be expected to follow the "chain of command." Employment to administrative positions would involve high levels of training and experience in "specializations" such as curriculum or finance. Advancement (promotion) would be influenced significantly by seniority, not necessarily by meritorious performance.

Partly because it denies a need to interact with external forces, the bureaucratic organization views conflict as an evil which is to be ignored or eradicated (Owens, 1981). Goal setting, the use of rigid, written school board policies and regulations, and authority control also would be common attributes of this operational design.

Quantitative measures of assessment would be advocated virtually for every function and person within the school district (Hamm and Brown, 1979). The focus of such an evaluation usually would be summative rather than formative: separating the "producers" and "nonproducers" in order to dismiss the unproductive employees would be the prime goal of the process. In these closed settings, performance evaluation rarely is viewed as a technique instituted with the express purpose of improving the employee.

Closed systems are most efficient when the environment is calm. A tranquil environment has little or no conflict (turmoil). As a result, very few external demands are placed upon the organization. All types of conflict are abhorred in a bureaucracy, and management is conditioned to act swiftly to remove it. Risk taking is considered foolish and disruptive; as a result, management that avoids failure is looked upon favorably. Status and role identification are strengthened and become extremely important to administrators under such conditions (Bassett, 1970).

The school board in an impervious system would place value upon technical skills as selection criteria for employment to administrative positions. Managerial competencies in finance, personnel, and evaluation exemplify expertise commonly cited. Direct interference into executive functions is perceived as a deterrent to efficiency. Because administrators are viewed as technical experts, extending the power for decisions to nonadministrative staff is perceived as an unnecessary political act.

Communication systems also are affected by closed structure. The writing of memoranda and the exclusive use of prescribed lines of communication are common. Formal titles are important and appear in both verbal and written communications. Expected conformity becomes a controlling factor, and it extends even to areas such as administrative apparel (one's personal appearance should be appropriate for one's level of authority).

Burearcracy in Other Contexts

The previous description of the bureaucratic school system serves to exemplify the features of a closed model for a human-intensive, professionally dominated, public, service organization. Accordingly, this information is applicable to agencies similar in purpose and composition (such as hospitals and mental health clinics). Agencies having significantly different purposes need to be studied from a different perspective. For example, private businesses, industry, proprietary schools, and the military are agencies in which adult education occurs and in which the existence of bureaucratic behaviors may have fewer negative effects. Private ventures have less demand to interact with their environment: as such, they can tolerate a more closed organizational climate.

The essential point is that bureaucracy, or attributes thereof, may permeate the structure, operations, and purpose of any organization that opts to engage in adult education. In this regard, the practitioner must understand the components and potential effects of bureaucratic design and how this design may advance or hinder educational program development. For example, conflict usually occurs when an organization's needs are incongruent with the needs of individuals in the organization. An understanding of organizational behavior increases the likelihood that the administrator will be prepared to cope with these occurrences.

The Strengths and Weaknesses of the Bureaucracy

As mentioned previously, many persons equate bureaucracy with something evil, sinister, and inefficient. Yet, under certain circumstances, classical theory can be very effective (Robbins, 1976). Organizations embracing bureaucratic practices, for example, can identify more clearly levels of responsibility and authority. Particularly in large enterprises, the highly structured format frequently reduces tasks to a less complex level, which tends to make the job requirements more manageable. The standardization of procedures also may be viewed by some as a positive attribute.

The failure to recognize the needs of individual workers and the segregation of the organization from external environments, however, result in a myriad of negative outcomes for the highly bureaucratic public institution. Hanson (1979) identifies the following weaknesses of a bureaucracy:

> Closed systems deter the process of change.
>
> Mock, representative, and punishment-centered rules become the norm.
>
> Because of rigidity, there is often a failure to provide for the unexpected.
>
> The high use of rules tends to establish minimum performance levels as acceptable levels of performance.
>
> The hierarchical structure is conducive to the "filtering" of derogatory or critical information as communications are processed.

In professionally dominated organizations (organizations in which the work force is composed of a majority of professionals), the bureaucratic model produces essential concerns. Bennis (1966) pointed out that bureaucracies do not provide adequately for individual growth, and this deficiency is especially enervating for the professional employee. Preservice education for most professionals stresses the qualities of independent and peer decision making. When highly educated employees are denied this opportunity, they tend to react negatively.

The strict adherence to rules often creates an atmosphere in which tasks become more important than people. Since adult education is a process focusing upon people, this attribute of the bureaucracy is most significant. Campbell et al. (1980) identify two shortcomings that relate to the development of educational programs:

> The whole concept of a hierarchy presents a picture contrary to the American commitment to egalitarianism.
>
> The control structure of bureaucracies is contrary to the orientation of professional groups. Professional groups usually adopt voluntary forms of control, and teachers, for example, may find the rigid rules demeaning.

Even though bureaucratic structure may function more effectively in private enterprise, general operational standards may not be environmentally suitable if a private company wishes to engage in adult education. Potential conflicts between efficiency and service and the competing needs of the organization and the individuals who interact with the organization exemplify potential pitfalls for any agency that ventures into organized adult learning programs.

THE SOCIOPOLITICAL SYSTEM

Sociopolitical theory recognizes the existence of many and varied social groups within an organization that exert power and influence over the goals, operations, and outcomes of the organization. In today's world, labor unions, community pressure groups, political factions, and the like represent the multitude of internal and external forces penetrating the boundaries of organizational decisions.

The Origins of Sociopolitical Theory

Early theorists often ignored the needs of individuals in studying organizational behavior. In doing so, they failed to explore the dynamics of group behavior. For example, could an informal group of employees affect the direction, functioning, or work atmosphere of an organization? The disregard for social and psychological aspects of formal organizations was a serious deficiency of the early theorists. The human element in production and other areas of organizational life was overlooked (Owens, 1981). Furthermore, there was no recognition of the organization as a culture—an entity with values, customs, rituals, and the like.

A major research study which provided insight into the question of the effects of group behavior was conducted during the period of 1927 to 1932 by Elton Mayo. Known as the Hawthorne Studies (because they were conducted at the Hawthorne Works of Western Electric Company near Chicago), this research revealed the tendency of workers to act and react as members of subgroups (Hanson, 1979). Prior to these findings most theorists believed that workers acted solely as individuals and that the primary sources of worker motivation and morale were salary and working conditions. The Hawthorne Studies concluded that the socialization of workers within an organization was certainly a dynamic force. The discovery of informal groups and the analysis of formal groups were significant contributions to organizational theory. One of the primary values of this information was the attention given to the differences between organizational and group goals (that is, the goals formulated by individuals who hold membership in a group).

Katz and Kahn (1966) point out the fallacy of equating the purposes or goals of organizations with those of individuals. In their classic book, *The Social Psychology of Organizations,* the authors identify ways in which informal subgroups affect the needs and behavior of individuals in the organization. This view of an organization as a social system is a radical departure from classical theory. In many ways it identifies each organization as unique and therefore not adaptable to universal imperatives espoused by burearcratic theorists.

The thrust of social theory is to explore the ways in which an organization really functions. This again is in contrast to classical theory, which is often criticized for concentrating upon the "ideal" method of operation. Getzels and Guba (1957) describe organizations as social systems with two major classes of phenomena, institutions and individuals. In their opinion, organizational behavior results from a blend of the institutional and individual motives. The foci of their work are the descriptions of individual and group behavior in certain organizational contexts.

The final component of sociopolitical theory involves the study of democratic organizations. Katz and Kahn (1966) contrast the nature of a democratic organization with the hierarchical model of the bureaucracy. The pyramid-shaped structure, as mentioned earlier, clearly distinguishes power levels. Power in a bureaucracy is highly concentrated, and it is associated with both executive and legislative functions. Thus, the chief executive not only exerts power in carrying out rules, but also may exert tremendous power over the function of formulating policy.

The democratic organization, on the other hand, distributes power, particularly legislative power. Political solutions, the use of coercion and compromise, are commonplace in the democratic organization. A number of theorists (Cyert and March, 1963; Allison, 1971; Pfeffer, 1981) have explored political models of decision making and their impact upon organizations. For example, this exploration has exhibited how concentrated power and shared power are two very different standards affecting organizational behavior.

The fusion of research focusing on worker and group behavior, the development of social systems theory, and the studies of political dynamics in organizations resulted in the formulation of sociopolitical theory. This theory describes and predicts organizational behavior on the basis of the study of individuals, subgroups, and decision-making processes that actually exist within a given organization.

The Use of Sociopolitical Theory

The emergence of unions exemplifies the potential for employee groups to amass power in an organization. Many administrators encounter the reality that formal groups such as unions and informal groups such as neighbor-hood coalitions exercise significant impact over legislative and executive authority. The acceptance of these groups (and their power) conditions the methods of leadership in any enterprise. In describing the sociopolitical school system, for example, Hanson (1979) cites the following observable characteristics:

A coalition of sociopolitical groups often functioning outside the formal system

The diffusion of power among groups

Control often emerging from informal group norms

Subordinates frequently managing superiors

Conflict frequently being functional

In this type of system, the leader must be skilled in using compromise. He or she must be able to identify clearly power structures and to be active politically within the organization. The authoritarian, "expert" model of the administrator promoted in classical theory is definitely misplaced in this context. Management in sociopolitical theory is directed toward achieving synthesis, coordination, and conflict resolution among organizational groups and individuals possessing varying interests, needs, and goals.

The use of representative committees would be a common aspect of the sociopolitical context. This method of decision making exposes the bias that political process is as important as the product. Efficiency might be sacrificed for high levels of employee involvement, and compromise is the most frequently used vehicle for resolving issues.

Strengths and Weaknesses of the Sociopolitical Theory

Sociopolitical theory recognizes the effects of individuals and groups upon organizational behavior. Likewise, it accepts the inevitability of the influence exerted by individuals and groups. Therefore, sociopolitical theory provides a framework that permits the detailed study of organizational behavior. Perhaps the greatest strength of this theory is its acceptance of conflict as a potential catalyst for organizational growth. Within this sociopolitical framework, organizational conflict is accepted as inevitable. Conflict is assigned a neutral value. Its ultimate effects are deemed to be a product of conflict management. Thus, conflict can, and often does, serve a functional purpose for the organization. This enlightened view is an asset. For example, recognizing that individual needs and organizational needs with regard to adult education are incongruent could lead to decisions benefiting both the individuals and the organization.

The use of compromise mandates that organizations maintain a high degree of flexibility. The reliance upon "win-win" strategies for conflict (as opposed to "win-lose") also is perceived as a strength of the sociopolitical system. This strategy allows people to participate and reach decisions without one party being defeated. Such an outcome can be observed in situations where adult education provides positive outcomes for the organization and its individual members. Less emphasis is placed upon legitimate power and authority to reach critical decisions.

Many managers remain dubious of accepting the operational aspects of sociopolitical theory. Among the more common fears are the following:

Recognizing groups such as unions allows them to become more powerful.

Political compromises often result in lower-quality decisions.

If managers rely upon compromise and create a wider base of shared power, they will be criticized for not maintaining control.

Allowing any form of shared governance in organizations is frequently interpreted as "weak" leadership by some control-minded critics. Therefore, not all enterprises may be objective about the realities of sociopolitical theory. Yet denial of the interactive aspects of individuals and groups predisposes administrators to certain problems which they may not understand. An out-of-hand rejection, likewise, does not diminish the potency of this theory, which has been accumulated through years of research.

A noted weakness of theories which view organizations as social systems is the restricted view they provide. In recent years, theorists have recognized that institutions consist of more than individuals, informal groups, formal groups, goals, and the like. The nature of tasks and technology are two additional factors which interact to affect behavior (Owens, 1981). Given the rapid expansion of science, these overlooked factors are becoming more prominent. Moreover, the cultural elements of institutions receive little attention.

Some scholars have observed that overemphasis on human needs could be deleterious to the goals of the organization. The desire to appease employees may result in a form of organizational dysfunction. Keeping institutional goals in balance with individual employee needs is a complex task. Misunderstandings in applying sociopolitical theory could result in an imbalance in these goals and needs.

OPEN SYSTEMS THEORY

Open systems theory focuses upon the interaction between the organization and its external environment. This theory presents a third distinct alternative for studying, understanding, and predicting organizational behavior. In viewing the organization as more than structure and people, this theory views behavior within a sociotechnical system.

Closely associated with this concept of open systems theory is contingency theory. Hellriegel and Slocum (1976) identify contingency theory as a new and innovative way to analyze interrelationships in an organization. Open systems theory and contingency theory reject the notion that organizations are static. A constant interaction with the environment spawns a need for creativity and flexibility in leadership. In a dynamic society, the attributes of leadership (deciding the right things to do) become more critical than management (doing things the right way). Given the world today, open systems theory is growing in popularity.

The Origins of Open Systems Theory

One of the pioneers of open systems theory was Floyd H. Allport. Allport (1954) believed that the essence of understanding social behavior involved an analysis of continuous interactions which provided cycles of events. His model is very similar to the general systems theory model developed by biologist Ludwig von Bertalonffy.

General systems theory focuses upon the biological interdependence of cells within an organism and the interdependence of molecules within a cell. By substituting organization for organism, groups for cells, and individuals for molecules, one attains insight into the potential application of this theory for studying institutions (Owens, 1981). The organization is composed of individuals and groups, and each component is dependent: that is, each element of the organization is related to other elements. The relationships are quite similar to the basic functions within human biology. For example, a decision in marketing may have serious implications for personnel—similar to the way a virus attacking one part of the body may affect all body functions.

Open systems theory identifies the prevalence of certain patterns of cyclical interaction in all organizations. However, it does not validate the premise that there is one best organizational pattern or prevalent method of decision making. Rather, it advocates the pragmatic position of establishing situational contingencies to cope with an ever-changing environment.

As previously indicated, relating open systems theory to contingency theory is now common practice. Laurence and Lorsh (1967) perceive open systems as organizations capable of altering interrelationships and practices that depend upon environmental influences and demands. Thus, unlike the bureaucracy with its rigid approach, the open organization bases its response, decision, control, and so forth on knowledge of its interrelationships and the context in which an issue evolves. The resulting leadership behavior is eclectic and situational.

Open systems theory also includes the concepts of differentiation and integration. Differentiation is defined as the difference in knowledge and skills of individuals, and integration refers to the ability to unify efforts. Laurence and Lorsh (1967) maintain that the higher the levels of differentiation and integration, the better equipped is the organization to cope with an unstable environment. Thus, diversity in individual worker skills and the ability to fuse these skills to meet specific objectives are necessary attributes of an effective open system. The concept of project management (where special teams are formulated to resolve specific issues) is an excellent example of high differentiation and integration. Unlike the bureaucracy, in which tasks are assigned to a division of the organization according to the technical identity in that division, project management seeks the talents of individuals appropriate for the tasks and attempts to coordinate those talents regardless of the location of the individuals within the organization. For example, studying ways of cutting the budget might be assigned solely to fiscal operations in a bureaucracy. In an open system, a special committee might be formed to bring together many and varied skills, viewpoints, and philosophies. This is done because the organization believes that budget cuts will affect all operations.

The Use of Open Systems Theory

An organization embracing an open systems concept would seek to identify cycles of interactions that take place between the various components of the system. For example, the relationship of principals to teachers in a school district would constitute a cycle of events. The power in the organization would be diffused among the various interacting groups; therefore, the interrelationships are of obvious importance because they create bonds of dependency. Thus, workers rely upon the manager's power at certain times, and at other times, the manager is dependent upon the workers. At times the manager may be authoritarian; or she or he may rely upon compromise; or she or he may remain passive. The situation dictates the appropriate behavior. The bond (or cycle) plays a vital role in establishing the parameters for alternatives.

The more open an organization and the higher the levels of differentiation and integration, the more capable the system is of coping with conflict and change created by turbulence in the environment. In fact, conflict may be viewed as an opportunity to change directions, to alter programs and procedures, and to seek improvements. This view of conflict partially explains why open institutions frequently are better able to cope with conflict than are closed institutions. For example, open organizations may cope with collective bargaining more effectively. High levels of differentiation and integration provide the organization with an assortment of technical skills, values, viewpoints, educational backgrounds, and experiences. Because this variety exists, the organization possesses a larger pool of resources.

The administrators in an open system avoid rigidity. The idea that there is "one best way" to manage, to reach decisions, to plan programs, or to supervise is considered irrational. The organization exerts an effort to establish a network for interaction with internal and external forces. Through this communication process, input is welcomed from constituents of the organization and from components of the external environment.

The administrator is a director of interaction, integration, and adaptation. He or she maintains a positive, visible image in the organization and community. Flexibility, eclectic approaches to management, and the ability to listen are prized attributes of leadership in an open system. The administrator should be a skilled facilitator.

The Strengths and Weaknesses of Open Systems Theory

There is little doubt that open systems theory observes the greatest amount of flexibility in management. In developing adult education, this flexibility will often be a strength. The theory is compatible with the ideals of democratic governance, an asset particularly cogent to public, service organizations. Again, this is especially noteworthy with reference to adult education in which practitioners need to be sensitive to the needs and desires of learners, the organization, and society.

Most scholars agree that conflict is inevitable for all organizations. Open systems theory provides a positive approach to encountering conflict. The rejection of confined principles of management allows adaptations to changes in philosophy, missions, public demand, and environmental needs. The organization is not reliant upon the exclusive use of authority or the exclusive use of compromise to execute leadership. All factors which may affect outcomes are studied in an integrated approach to planning and decision making.

There are obvious similarities between sociopolitical and open systems theories. To this extent, the weaknesses stated for the sociopolitical theory are applicable here. In addition, the effective use of open systems theory requires expertise which may be lacking in many organizations. The effectual implementation of a contingency approach relies upon creative individuals who accept the concept of interdependency between the organization and its environs. Individuals, particularly administrators, should exhibit the willingness and ability to be flexible in missions and practices so that leadership decisions based upon theoretical study will not be impaired by personal bias. Formal academic preparation in the behavioral sciences appears to be advantageous for effective leadership in open settings.

PUTTING THEORY INTO PRACTICE

Every educational operation in America confronts the problem of existing in a pluralistic and changing society. The choices for administering the present and planning the future are clear. The administrator may choose to repeat the practices observed in other institutions; he or she may choose to pursue a process of trial and error; or he or she may choose to function within the parameters of a conceptual framework and strategy. When the last alternative is selected, the concept of organizational development strategy is adopted.

Schmuck et al. (1977) describe an organizational development strategy as a mechanism to help educational enterprises become self-correcting, self-renewing, and receptive to change. Relying upon empirical data that systematically examine practices and outcomes increases the probability that the institution will be able to respond to conflict with innovative and integrated management approaches.

The study of organizational theory exposes the administrator to recurring patterns of behavior which become invaluable to leadership. The overemphasis on product, people, or process may result in organizational dysfunctions. The research and writing of scholars from the varied behavioral sciences provide a realistic framework for the student and practitioner of adult education leadership.

Designing adult education programs requires some degree of sophistication in general administration. This knowledge base includes information on organizational dynamics. Since adult programs may be created in a multitude of settings, this knowledge of organizational theory serves two purposes. First, the educational leader benefits from understanding the organization in which he or she is employed—the parent organization. Second, organizational knowledge provides the leader with a framework for developing an organizational entity (that is, an adult education program) within an organization (a school district, college, military, private enterprise, etc.). Since organizations are heterogeneous (exhibit weighty differences), all three theories of organizations presented in this chapter may have relevance for the adult education practitioner. Since theory is a representation of reality, the selection of the appropriate theory is dictated by the organizational climate in which the adult educator is placed.

SUMMARY

This chapter reviewed three organizational theories about developing adult education programs. The theories describe the interactions of individuals and groups with the organization and the organization's relationship with its environment. The three theories also represent a form of evolution of information about organizational behavior.

Theories provide a framework of reality. To the administrator of adult education, they offer a potential tool for effective program planning. By infusing this tool into the process of making decisions, leaders put themselves in a position to make more informed decisions. To make good decisions, the adult education administrator must be able to apply the knowledge of organizational theory in the real world.

If administrators dismiss theory as inapplicable, they seriously reduce their ability to direct the future of education. In the absence of direction, fortuitous elements will prevail in determining the institution's destiny. Since adult education may exist in myriad settings, understanding organizational dynamics is a particularly important attribute. It allows the person to select the appropriate theory to apply in practice.

FOR FURTHER DISCUSSION

1. The term *bureaucracy* connotes inefficiency and insensitivity to many people. Why has this perception emerged? Is it an accurate perception?

2. Discuss the issue of "rationality" as it applies to organizational design and functions.

3. The social views of organization include the belief that organizational behavior is a blend of institutional and individual motives. Discuss the application of this belief to an adult education program.

4. Contrast the use of power (and types of power used) in the bureaucratic organization and the sociopolitical organization.

5. Adult education programs may exist in a myriad of environments. Does this mean that an effective adult education program can exist in either an open or closed organization? Why or why not?

6. An adult education program functioning as a subunit of a public school district is subject to the same amount of environmental turmoil as is an inservice program operated by a large, private corporation (such as General Motors or Westinghouse). Defend or refute this statement.

7. Since public institutions are to some degree open institutions, and since a high percentage of adult education programs are operated by public institutions (that is, funded by public tax dollars), it would not be advantageous to educate adult education administrators with the same curricula used to educate business executives (for example, with M.B.A. curricula). Defend or refute this statement.

8. If an adult education administrator is a firm believer in open organizations and contingency management, what, if any, problems would he or she incur if employed in a leadership position in a highly bureaucratic organization?

REFERENCES

Allison, G. T. (1971). *Essence of decision.* Boston: Little, Brown and Company.

Allport, F. H. (1954). The structuring of events: Outline of a general theory with application to psychology. *Psychological Review, 61,* 281–303.

Bassett, G. A. (1970). Leadership style and strategy. In L. A. Netzer, G. G. Eye, A. Graef, R. D. Krey, and J. F. Overman (Eds.), *Interdisciplinary foundations of supervision* (pp. 221–231). Boston: Allyn and Bacon

Bennis, W. S. (1966). Organizational developments and the fate of bureaucracy. *Industrial Management Review, 7*(2), 41–55.

Callahan, R. E. (1962). *Education and the cult of efficiency.* Chicago: University of Chicago Press.

Campbell, R. F., Cunningham, L. L., Nystrand, R. O., and Usdan, M. D. (1980). *The organization and control of American schools.* Columbus, OH: Charles E. Merrill.

Carver, F. D., and Sergiovanni, T. J. (1969). *Organization and human behavior: Focus on schools.* New York: McGraw-Hill.

Cyert, R. M., and March, J. G. (1963). *A behavioral theory of the firm.* Englewood Cliffs, NJ: Prentice-Hall.

Getzels, J. W., and Guba, E. G. (1957). Social behavior and the administrative process. *The School Review, 65,* 423–441.

Hamm, R., and Brown, G. (1979). Educational bureaucracy: What to do about it? *Clearing House, 53,* 40–43.

Hanson, E. M. (1979). *Educational administration and organizational behavior.* Boston: Allyn and Bacon.

Harper, D. (1965). The growth of bureaucracies in school systems. *American Journal of Economics and Sociology, 24,* 261–272.

Hellriegel, D., and Slocum, J. W., Jr. (1976). *Organizational behavior: Contingency views.* St. Paul, MN: West Publishing Company.

Katz, D., and Kahn, R. (1966). *The social psychology of organizations.* New York: John Wiley.

Laurence, P. R., and Lorsh, J. W. (1967). *Organization and environment.* Homewood, IL: Richard Irwin.

Malinowski, B. (1960). *A scientific theory of culture and other essays.* New York: Galaxy-Oxford University Press.

March, J. G. (1984). How we talk and how we act: Administrative theory and administrative life. In T. Sergiovanni and J. Corablly (Eds.), *Leadership and organizational culture* (pp. 18–35). Urbana, IL: University of Illinois Press.

March, J. G., and Simon, H. A. (1958). *Organizations.* New York: John Wiley.

Owens, R. F. (1981). *Organizational behavior in education.* Englewood Cliffs, NJ: Prentice-Hall.

Pfeffer, J. (1981). *Power in organizations.* Marshfield, MA: Pitman Publishing.

Robbins, S. P. (1976). *The administrative process: Integrating theory and practice.* Englewood Cliffs, NJ: Prentice-Hall.

Schmuck, A., Runkel, P. J., Arends, J. H., and Arends, R. I. (1977). *The second handbook of organization development in schools.* Palo Alto, CA: Mayfield Publishing Company.

Szczypkowski, R. (1980). Objectives and activities. In Alan B. Knox (Ed.), *Developing, administering, and evaluating adult education* (pp. 37–74). San Francisco: Jossey-Bass.

Weber, M. (1947). *The theory of social and economic organizations* (Henderson and Parsons, Trans.), T. Parsons (Ed.). New York: The Free Press.

Yeshewalul, A., and Griffith, W. (1984). Agricultural extension workers' roles in Canada and the United States. *Adult Education Quarterly, 34*(4), 97–122.

CHAPTER 6

Applying Organizational Theory to Adult Education

The two previous chapters have discussed the essence of theory and have presented three prevalent theories of organizations. This chapter is devoted to applying organizational theory to the real world of adult education. In doing so, it uses the typology presented in chapter 3.

Most organizations, including those engaged in adult education, are complex. Some obviously are more complex than others. One major problem resulting from complexity is organizational uncertainty; a second problem is the development of an appropriate strategy to cope with this uncertainty (Thompson, 1967). Given this complexity and uncertainty planning and actualizing adult education programs are extremely difficult tasks. For many practitioners incertitude about structure, community support, and even the adult learner is a real problem.

March and Simon (1958) have pointed out that organizational uncertainty raises the risks of leadership, particularly in decision making. Ambiguity in philosophy, mission, structure, purpose, curricula, and so forth often requires the administrator of adult education to make guesses regarding what will be successful now and in the future. Vagueness is increased by the realization that each organization is really a mixture of four separate perspectives. These perspectives, or concepts, are often incongruent. They include the manifest organization (the concept of the organization illustrated on the line and staff chart of the organization), the assumed organization (the individual's perceptions of the organization), the extant organization (the organization as portrayed by systematic study and analysis by, say, an outside consultant), and the requisite organization (a portrayal of the organization if it were in accord with the reality of the situation within which it exists). Although ideally one would like these four concepts to be aligned, this rarely is the case. For this reason alone, certain levels of uncertainty can be found in every organization (Bennis, 1983).

Frequently, when confronted with high levels of uncertainty, leaders make adjustments (social, psychological, managerial adjustments) to protect their well-being. One common adjustment in these instances is the "uncertainty avoidance" syndrome. Cyert and March (1963) describe this behavior as the manager's obsession with short-range problems where prediction is less necessary or risky. When this occurs, unfortunately, long-range decision making suffers, and the results may be deleterious for the organization. Again, the dynamic nature of contemporary society needs to be accentuated. Long-range planning becomes even more critical when the future is quite uncertain.

The ambiguity of program development in adult education is often increased by the fact that many current administrators in this specialization are transplants from other sectors of human services occupations. In public schools, for example, it is not uncommon for the director of adult education to lack specific formal education or experience in administration or adult educa-tion (for example, a former high school teacher). Former agriculture or other vocational education teachers frequently are selected to fill these positions (Roudebush and Fallon, 1984).

One other consideration with regard to programming relates to role conflict. In simple terms, role conflict entails the differing expectations placed on one's performance. For example, the president of a company may have a set of expectations for a director of adult education, the director may have his or her own expectations, clients may have another set of expectations, and so forth. When these expectations are incongruent, role conflict emerges. Recent research in adult education exhibits the manner in which this conflict occurs and its negative effects.

Given these and other conditions previously discussed in this book, the germaneness of organizational theory to program development in adult educa-tion ought to be clear. The application of theory requires that the practitioner not only exhibit the ability to identify the variables present in a given situa-tion, but also to be able to identify the potential effects of those variables. In that decision making in the areas of strategic planning and policy is probably the most important task of top-level administrators (Yukl, 1981), the ability to apply theory in complex organizations is crucial.

VARIABLES RELATED TO THE USE OF ORGANIZATIONAL THEORY

Variables related to a given situation in which adult education is con-templated or actually offered can be divided into two major categories. The first includes variables which exist in the general environment, the setting outside of the organization. This setting might be a community, state, or region of the country. The second category includes variables present within the organization. It would be virtually impossible to develop exhaustive lists of these variables in this book; however, a select number of variables are provided as examples.

Environmental Variables

As previously noted, organizations do not exist in isolation. Rather, they exist within identifiable environs (Campbell, Corbally, and Nystrand, 1983). Scholars often refer to those surroundings as the "environmental field." The environment in this respect is not restricted to the physical abundance, but also includes values, needs, social issues, and other related factors.

Katz and Kahn (1978) have identified five major forces in the environmental field of an organization. These include the *cultural* force (for example, the ethnic composition of the community), the *political* force (such as community support for adult education), the *economic* force (such as available environmental fiscal support to offer or continue adult programs), the *informational and technical* force (such as available technology and the expertise to use it), and the *physical* force (adequate environmental conditions, such as populations, to support adult education). These factors combine to influence decisions made by the organization. Before applying theoretical constructs to program planning, the administrator benefits from having an accurate assessment of each of these environmental field factors.

Environmental fields also can be plotted on four continua, as shown below (adapted from work by Katz and Kahn in *The Social Psychology of Organizations* [1978]):

Stability ——————— Turbulence
Homogeneity ——————— Diversity
Clustering ——————— Randomness
Munificence ——————— Scarcity

Stability and turbulence refer to the intensity of problems created in the environmental field. A stable environment generates very little conflict or pressures that require the organization to make adjustments. Conversely, a turbulent environment begets high levels of conflict. For these reasons, open, flexible organizations function more effectively in turbulent environments. As an example, assume that a community formulates a political position that the public schools ought to be providing more and better programs for adults. The more open (and flexible) the organization of the school district, the more readily it is likely to respond to these environmental pressures. This is true for two primary reasons: the district is engaging in active communication with the environment, and the district maintains flexibility, which allows it to make rapid adjustments.

Homogeneity and diversity of the environmental field refer to the degree to which elements in the environment are similar. This similarity may relate to the ethnic origins of the population, the occupations of the population, the values of the population, the income levels of the population, and so forth. The greater the homogeneity, the easier it is for the organization to identify and understand the needs of the environment because commonalities typically cause the population to desire and need similar things. Open, flexible organizations tend to be more effective in environments with high levels of diversity where desires and needs tend to be complex and susceptible to change.

Clustering and randomness are used to describe the degree to which the environmental field is highly structured. High levels of randomness would indicate anarchy. The more uncertain or unpredictable the environmental field, the greater the demand for an organization to be flexible to respond to the needs and desires emanating from the external elements. Some communities are highly structured. They are blessed with networks of agencies which work in harmony. In these situations, degrees of closed climates can be more readily tolerated.

Lastly, scarcity and munificence identify the wealth of resources in the environmental field. An abundance of resources (money, materials, human resources) reduces the pressure upon the organization to be creative and adaptive. A YMCA existing in a munificent environment, for example, may meet the demand for a new course for adults in computer literacy simply by obtaining sufficient public donations to do so. A YMCA in a scarce environment, on the other hand, may be forced to redefine priorities and to drop some other programs(s) to secure the resources necessary to offer this course. The latter situation obviously requires more organizational flexibility and adjustment.

Organizational Variables

Proper application of organizational theory also requires an understanding of internal variables (those within the boundaries of the organization). Table 6-1 provides a profile of some of the more relevant factors which exist as organizational variables; however, this is not an exhaustive list. Often unique elements are present which require the practitioner to make considerations beyond the common variables listed here.

Table 6-1

Common Variables for Organizations

ITEM	RANGE	EXPLANATION
Size	Small–large	Number of persons in the organization
Purpose	Simple–complex	The mission(s) of the organization (such as single purpose versus multipurpose)
Expertise	Low–high	Special talents (such as leadership skills)
Resources	Low–high	Material goods, money, etc.
Differentiation	Low–high	Differentiation in job responsibilities and worker skills
Integration	Low–high	Ability to integrate human and physical resources to solve problems, plan, etc.
Employee types	Nonprofessional–professional	The degree to which the organization is composed of professionals
Philosophy of adult education	Person centered–organization centered	The reasons that adult education is provided
Networking	Isolated–highly integrated	The degree to which the organization cooperates with other agencies
Authority	Loose-knit–structured	The degree to which power and authority are concentrated
Climate	Open–closed	The degree to which the organization interacts with its environment

Each variable identifies characteristics of the organization, but again, the list in table 6-1 is not exhaustive. Still other variables may be unique to a given situation; where present, they should be included for purposes of analysis. The application of theory to program design is enhanced when the environmental field and organization are described accurately. They can be described by plotting variables on continua such as those presented in this chapter. The result of this effort is a profile which facilitates the use of theory. In essence, a visual image of the environmental field and the organization provides an informational footing for the use of theory.

TYPE A ORGANIZATIONS

Using the system developed in chapter 3, the remainder of this chapter explores the application of theory based upon the genre of the sponsoring institution. Type A organizations within this classification system are entities existing to serve adults. The primary (or even exclusive) mission is adult education. Examples of Type A organizations include proprietary schools (such as trade schools), consulting firms, residential adult centers, and nonresidential adult centers (Schroeder, 1970). There are two variables of particular import with regard to applying organizational theory to Type A institutions. The first is public versus private control, and the second is mission.

Public versus Private Control

Proprietary schools are privately owned and managed. At first glance, one might assume that this status would negate requirements for these organizations to interact with their environment, since private ventures can do as they please. The need to attract students and to generate profit is, however, a compelling influence which typically results in high levels of interaction between the organization and its environment. In fact, private ventures often are quite flexible because they may lose their attractiveness to consumers unless they are open to change.

A major difference between public and private Type A organizations is the manner in which environmental interaction is initiated. Public organizations usually are placed under the jurisdiction of boards of control; thus citizens have inroads for filing complaints, requesting changes, and so forth. As a result, regardless of administrative direction, environmental interaction (at some level) is inevitable in public organizations. By contrast, private ventures are much more dependent upon leadership initiatives to generate involvement with the environmental field. The control of the organization (ownership) may not be amenable to environmental interaction.

One should not conclude that environmental interaction is not necessary in private organizations. Monitoring needs and wants, for example, is a critical process for Type A institutions. The practitioner in the private sector often has the responsibility of initiating such interaction; because unlike in the public realm, such interventions are not inevitable. Given the necessity of generating income via satisfying consumer demands, total isolation from influences external to the parent organization could prove fatal.

Mission

One advantage of Type A organizations is the narrowness of mission. These enterprises have the sole purpose of providing education to adults. Private ventures may be established as either profit or nonprofit organizations, and profit enterprises obviously have a second mission of making money. Simplicity of function reduces the complexity of using theory.

Type A organizations can meld the tenets of adult education with those of program design with greater ease because fewer internal variables exist. Thus, allowing high levels of learner input into adult programming as prescribed by many scholars (for example, Knowles, 1982) does not set precedent or jeopardize procedures for other segments of the organization. Discussion related to other types of enterprises will illuminate the complexity of theoretical applications where missions are quite heterogeneous.

Perhaps the greatest leadership error of proprietary schools is the myopic belief that private enterprise can and should function as a closed institution. As better-educated adult leaders enter positions in these types of operation, this problem should diminish. Those institutions expressing a knowledge of theory, a sensitivity for the needs of their adult clients, and a format for assessing these needs in the environment are more likely to be successful.

TYPE B ORGANIZATIONS

A large segment of adult education occurs in institutions which have the primary mission of serving youth. Public school systems (K–12), community colleges, colleges, and universities are included in this grouping of Type B organizations. These institutions are enterprises which provide adult education as a secondary funtion. The application of theory to adult program development is more complex in these settings than in Type A organizations. Nevertheless, Type B institutions do possess the commonality of an educational mission: that is, although they serve children and adults, their overall service is education. This characteristic can reduce ambiguity in program planning. The major components of Type B merit separate review.

Public School Systems

Adult programs offered by public school systems vary in scope and design. Most often these services are designed as evening courses; however, the concept of the full-time, twelve-month adult education center began growing in popularity in the 1960s (Finch, 1970). Often ignored with respect to adult education in public school systems is the issue of staff development. Inservice programs that are designed to increase employee skills and that are organized and sponsored by the school system are another common form of adult education.

Applying organizational theory to leadership of adult education in public school settings is an intricate task. A multitude of significant variables make planning, design, and administration especially critical. Some of the more important variables related to public schools are as follows:

Primacy of pedagogy. Because the primary audience is youth, there is a tendency to treat adult learners in the same manner as children.

Quasi-bureaucratic structure. Because school systems have evolved as quasi-bureaucracies, it is difficult to accept aspects of openness (such as adult learner participation, change, etc.)

Imposed mission. Some administrators believe that society forces school districts to offer adult education, and they question the validity of these services in public schools.

Expertise. Few employees have specific preparations to teach adults or to plan adult programs.

Resources. School systems often have limited resources, and allocations to secondary functions become extremely limited.

Designing adult programs in public schools entails planning an organization within an organization. As previously stressed, the administrator not only must be knowledgeable in adult education, but he or she must understand the dynamics of the parent institution. Since the proclivity of public schools is to resist change, that is, to act in a closed manner (Hanson, 1979), the task of the program planner is usually difficult. To institute programs which are highly individualized, which are unstructured in time elements, and which rely heavily upon learner input can be threatening to the organizational stability of many school systems.

Public schools, regardless of leadership direction, continuously are bombarded by demands from the environmental field (Kowalski, 1986). The existence of adult education in this context is illustrated in figure 6-1. What occurs in the adult programs is affected not only by the organizational design and the social and technical aspects of the parent institution, but also by turmoil in the environmental field. Thus in highly closed school systems, the existence of adult programs may be viewed as a necessary evil, and as just another source of potential conflict threatening the stability of the organization. Where adult education is perceived as a nuisance, energy will be expended to avoid it. As figure 6-1 indicates, environmental turmoil may affect the organization, the adult program, the learner, or all three simultaneously. The demand for a speed reading course for adults, for example, may put pressure upon the director of adult education, upon the superintendent and school board, or on the director of adult education, the superintendent, and the school board at the same time.

FIGURE 6-1

FOUR FACTORS AFFECTING ADULT EDUCATION

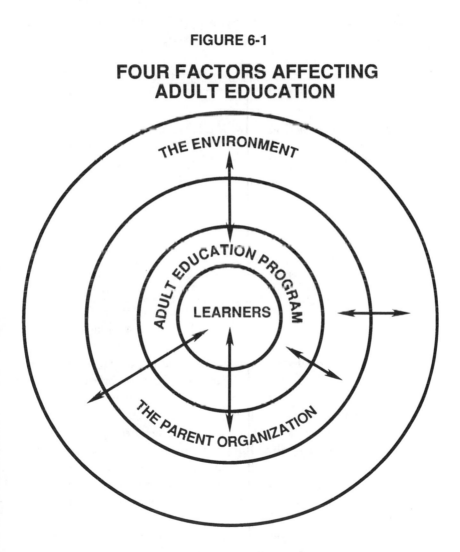

Higher Education

The term *higher education* is used to connote community colleges, colleges, universities, and independent professional schools (such as schools of medicine that are not a part of a university). Adult programs in these contexts are usually referred to as *continuing education*. As previously discussed in this book, accurate depictions of what constitutes adult education in colleges is difficult. It can range from basic literacy classes to special programs for upgrading the skills of surgeons.

Following are some of the important variables involved in adult education in higher education:

> *Public versus private control.* This issue concerns the degree to which the parent organization perceives a need to serve general public needs and to make programs profitable.
>
> *Continuing education mission.* The actual purpose of adult programs may vary from a genuine interest in helping people to generating added revenue for the institution (profit).
>
> *Governance structure.* Institutions exhibit tremendous differences in formal and informal decision making, openness, and so forth.
>
> *Overall mission.* Some institutions, such as public community colleges, have a direct mission to serve adult learners.
>
> *Program integration.* This is the degree to which continuing education programs are either infused or separated from other programs.
>
> *Resources.* These are the human and material resources available.

Haygood (1970) points out that the rapid growth of adult programs in colleges and universities did not indicate necessarily a major philosophical commitment. Often several dedicated individuals and the desire to find added revenues were the catalysts for such programs. This fact has subtle, if not direct, ramifications for continuing education units as they struggle to create congruence between educational and financial issues.

The tasks of organization and program planning are complicated further by a lack of uniformity. Basically, adult programs and services are offered either as an independent unit (such as a school of continuing education) or as a function of a multipurpose unit (such as a subpart of a college of education). This diversity in organizational design intensifies the burden of the planning procedure.

Community colleges typically have had less internal friction than four-year institutions in developing adult programs. This is true in large part because most community colleges (particularly those publicly controlled) accept a mission that extends far beyond formal, on-campus instruction for youth (Harlacher, 1970). Accordingly, the development and integration of adult programs have not met the resistance exhibited on the campuses of many traditional four-year institutions. Overall, however, a change in attitude about lifelong education is creating new opportunities for adults throughout higher education. Demographic realities also are causing most institutions of higher education to welcome "nontraditional" students.

TYPE C ORGANIZATIONS

Type C organizations include community service agencies which provide adult education as a corollary function. Examples include libraries, hospitals, mental health clinics, and museums. Although adult education is an allied function in these settings, it is embedded in the general mission to enhance community life.

Applying theory to Type C organizations is conditioned by the general variables discussed earlier in the chapter (size, governance, control). These organizations exhibit many similarities to Type B organizations (serving youth and adults, an organization within an organization), but one glaring exception is noted. Unlike educational institutions, these enterprises provide several services (such as health care and counseling). This feature makes Type C organizations even more likely to have low levels of expertise in adult education. Often the employees who are assigned to adult programs are persons who were employed for other agency services. Thus, a nurse or librarian may be asked to develop an adult program even though he or she may lack education or experience in adult education. For this reason, these organizations are usually more likely to link up with other community agencies to provide services. These linkages furnish the organization with some expertise that otherwise might not be available. For example, the YMCA, the city library, and the public school system might work together to offer a course in creative writing for senior citizens. Compatibility with the parent organization, willingness to work cooperatively with other agencies, and flexibility are characteristics to be considered by the adult education administrator working in a Type C organization. Because these programs are allied functions, design ought to interface successfully with the primary missions of the institution. Thus, the degree to which adult education creates conflict or financial stress for the primary organizational functions is a paramount factor in determining the scope of programs. An overly aggressive adult education administrator, for example, may threaten others in the organization to the point that adult programs suffer.

TYPE D ORGANIZATIONS

This category of organizations includes private businesses and private foundations. The common thread among these two institutions is that adult education is provided to serve the special interests of the organization or groups of its members. A large automobile manufacturer, for example, may provide learning programs to improve worker efficiency. These programs, often referred to as "training" or "staff development," are aimed at facilitating organizational goal attainment. Improving worker skills enhances productivity and organizational goal attainment. Private foundations, on the other hand, may be concerned with advancing knowledge related to philosophical positions and values. Providing courses for Bible study might be related to a religious mission of a foundation.

The application of theory in Type D organizations is based in large measure upon the climate existing in the organization as a whole. Private business ventures tend to have a closed posture toward the general environment. For this reason, change may not be readily instituted. The development of adult education within this climate must be executed with sensitivity to this condition.

Closed organizations also tend to be authority centered and to have a clearly visible hierarchical structure of leadership. The "chain of command" is sacred, and disruption is viewed as a negative factor diminishing operational efficiency. Essentially, Type D institutions tend to exhibit the characteristics of a bureaucracy. This fact can present a unique problem for adult education programming, which is often contrary to a closed climate (Mee and Wiltshire, 1978).

Following are some variables to be considered in program design and development in bureaucratic-type organizations.

> *Closed climate.* The purposes of adult education are dictated by the needs of the parent organization rather than by the needs of individuals or the external environment.
>
> *Hierarchy of authority.* High levels of learner input in planning probably would not occur, particularly when such participation is perceived as inefficient.
>
> *Rewards for participation.* Because participation is based upon organizational needs, rewards for the adult learner often are extrinsic rather than intrinsic.
>
> *Resources.* Since programs are designed to meet organizational needs, resources are available according to priorities within the total organization.
>
> *Leadership.* The nature of the organization will provide the adult education administrator with legitimate authority to run the program; however, the total program may be affected by its larger component (such as the entire personnel division).

Expertise. Frequently adult programs are developed without special assistance in adult education (training programs, materials, etc., are developed by personnel executives).

Evaluation. Improved goal attainment for the organization is the primary measure for success; thus evaluation will focus upon organizational goal attainment.

Environmental conditions are causing many closed organizations to rethink their attitudes toward change. For example, companies are becoming interested in the organizational values of Japanese manufacturers. Private businesses are beginning to realize that providing adult programs to serve employee interests also may be productive for the organization in the long term. If this perspective of indirect benefits continues to gain popularity, the design and development of adult programs in these institutions may become more dynamic and independent. The result would be more programs, greater diversity in program offerings, and less emphasis on corporate goal attainment as the sole measure for program continuance.

TYPE E ORGANIZATIONS

Included in Type E organizations are those enterprises which are voluntary in nature and which engage in adult education as a secondary function. Included would be labor unions, professional associations, pressure groups, service clubs, social clubs, churches, and recreational entities (such as the YMCA). The development of programs in these types of organizations can occur in a variety of climates. Labor unions, for example, could be structured quite bureaucratically and exhibit a closed climate. A service club, on the other hand, could be operated in an open fashion with power and decision making dispersed among the members of the organization.

Since membership in these organizations is voluntary, the planning of programs usually will be based upon needs which are commonly expressed by the members of the organization. A country club, for example, may organize classes in golf instruction because many members want the program. The application of theory to Type E institutions suggests that interaction within the parent organization is extremely important. Forces spawning adult programs frequently are related to the common attributes of the organizational members. For example, the American Medical Association offers courses in estate planning because many physicians need or desire to engage in that activity. Influences in the environment also can serve as catalysts for adult programming. New techniques in fund-raising may cause the Rotary Club to offer workshops for its members so they can be competitive in this function.

TYPE F ORGANIZATIONS

The final category of organizations includes governmental agencies which engage in forms of adult education. The military, the Department of Agriculture, prisons, and the local board of health are examples of agencies in this category. Adult programs are a secondary function for Type F organizations. Access to appropriate personnel and resources is a common problem for these agencies.

Frequently, adult programming in governmental agencies is designed to enhance the quality of the agency (for example, providing educational opportunities for soldiers improves the quality of the army). But programs focusing on the learner's needs are also common (for example, offering extension classes for farmers). Type F agencies tend to be bureaucratic in nature, exhibiting the attributes of authority common to private corporations. Thus, much of the discussion of Type D organizations is relevant here. Since Type F organizations can and do serve diverse needs, role conflict can be a problem for the practitioner. The clients may expect decisions which give primary consideration to their needs, and the organization may do likewise (Yeshewalul and Griffith, 1984).

SUMMARY

Adult education may occur in virtually any type of organizational setting. The use of theory which provides a framework for understanding behavior in varying types of organizational climates is a valuable tool to the adult education practitioner. It allows the administrator to predict expected reactions, successes, and so forth when program planning initiatives are considered.

Some organizations are highly bureaucratic and maintain a closed climate: that is, they avoid high levels of interaction with their environment. Other organizations are quite democratic. Power is shared by virtually everyone in the organization. The success of program planning in this type of setting often is based on conditions substantially different from those prevailing in the closed organization. Thus, planning procedures and decisions which succeed in one institution may fail in another.

Determining the organizational climate is a prerequisite to the successful application of organizational theory to adult education. This process is completed by examining a number of variables which provide a description of the organization and how it functions. This process is facilitated by using a typology.

FOR FURTHER DISCUSSION

1. List common environmental factors that have affected adult education positively and negatively.

2. Why have public school systems been expected to develop adult education programs?

3. Would it be a good idea for the best minds in adult education to gather and develop a single organizational plan which then could be used by any institution to develop and design programs? Why or why not?

4. List the organizational variables in an organization with which you are familiar (such as a YWCA, school district, college, etc.).

5. Are private proprietary schools more apt to change to meet environmental demands than are public institutions? Why or why not?

6. Why have public schools been resistant to change?

7. Discuss the advantages and disadvantages of organizing an adult program (continuing education) as a separate unit within an institution of higher education.

8. Contrast motivators for adult study in Type D organizations with those in other types of organizations.

REFERENCES

Bennis, W. (1983). *The chief.* New York: William Morrow.

Campbell, R. F., Corbally, J. E. and Nystrand, R. O. (1983). *Introduction to educational administration.* Boston: Allyn and Bacon.

Cyert, R., and March, J. G. (1963). *A behavioral theory of the firm.* Englewood Cliffs, NJ: Prentice-Hall.

Finch, R. E. (1970). Public schools. In R. M. Smith, G. F. Aker, and J. R. Kidd (Eds.), *Handbook of adult education* (pp. 231-243). New York: Macmillan.

Hanson, E. M. (1979). *Educational administration and organizational behavior.* Boston: Allyn and Bacon.

Harlacher, E. L. (1970). Community colleges. In R. M. Smith, G. F. Aker, and J. R. Kidd (Eds.), *Handbook of adult education* (pp. 213-229). New York: Macmillan.

Haygood, K. (1970). Colleges and universities. In R. M. Smith, G. F. Aker, and J. R. Kidd (Eds.), *Handbook of adult education* (pp. 191–212). New York: Macmillan.

Katz, D., and Kahn, R. L. (1978). *The social psychology of organizations.* New York: John Wiley.

Knowles, M. S. (1982). *The modern practice of adult education.* Chicago: Follett.

Kowalski, T. J. (1986). Adult education: The role of Public School districts. *Eastern Education Journal, 18*(2), 18-20.

March, J. G., and Simon, H. A. (1958). *Organizations.* New York: John Wiley.

Mee, G., and Wiltshire, H. (1978). *Structure and performance in adult education.* London: Longman.

Roudebush, D. M., and Fallon, J. A. (1984). A study of career patterns, professional mobility and job satisfaction levels among public school adult education administrators in Indiana. *Proceedings of the 25th Annual Adult Education Research Conference* (pp. 178–183). Raleigh, NC: Department of Adult and Community College Education, North Carolina State University.

Schroeder, W. L. (1970). Adult education defined and described. In R. M. Smith, G. F. Aker and J. R. Kidd (Eds.), *Handbook of adult education* (pp. 25–43). New York: Macmillan.

Thompson, J. D. (1967). *Organization in action.* New York: McGraw-Hill.

Yeshewalul, A., and Griffith, W. (1984). Agricultural extension workers' roles in Canada and the United States. *Adult Education Quarterly, 34*(4), 197–212.

Yukl, G. A. (1981). *Leadership in organizations.* Englewood Cliffs, NJ: Prentice-Hall.

PART III

The Planning Process

CHAPTER 7

Program Planning

By now it should be clear that planning programs for adults is a bit more complicated than most presume. Not only must the values, needs, interests, and wants of learners be addressed, but they usually must be considered in a manner which is congruent with the mission of the sponsoring organization. This is why an understanding of organizational dynamics is so important to the adult education practitioner. The best efforts of providing learning activities may be attenuated if the plans fail to comply with organizational philosophy, format, or functions. Or conversely, the client may be placed at a disadvantage if the organization totally dominates program planning.

Since organizations are unique entities, are there no universal principles for program planning? Does every organization require a novel approach to the preparation of adult education? Although organizations have their own identity, this fact does not diminish the value of proven principles for program planning. The key is the individualization of application—using the components within the organizational context. This chapter illuminates the need to use contingencies based upon the climate, mission, and priorities of the sponsoring institution, the needs and values of society, and the needs and values of adult learners. It is when sound principles are used in this manner that enlightened planning occurs.

COMPREHENSIVE VERSUS INDIVIDUAL PROGRAMS

Before discussing planning per se, it is helpful to clarify the meaning of the term *adult education program*. Often this term is confused with *curriculum*. Curriculum development is a subpart of program planning and relates only to the selection and sequencing of the learning experiences. A program is much broader and includes additional facets, such as budgeting, marketing, and evaluation. Schroeder (1970) points out that the concept of a program has been used to refer to many things, including the following:

- All the educational activities available to adults in a community
- The total adult education effort of a given agency
- The educational activities designed for segments of the population
- The social roles with which these activities are related
- The nature of a specific activity

Within the practice of adult education, the two most common uses of the term *program* relate to offerings within a given agency. The first is the concept of the *comprehensive program*. If one refers to all the adult education offered by an organization, one is talking about the comprehensive program. It is the sum of the various courses, experiences, and the like which are planned within the functions related to designed learning. The comprehensive program represents the macro view of planning. For example, a city hospital may offer a comprehensive program ranging from formal courses in weight control, to programmed learning packages for infant care, to tutoring for stroke recovery patients. Everything this hospital offers which is termed "adult education" should be bound together by a comprehensive program plan. Such a plan identifies the key factors, such as goals and objectives, which guide the formulation, operation, and evaluation of components of the total efforts classified as adult education.

Then there are the *individual programs*—the separate parts of the comprehensive program. A class in infant care is an individual program which is part of the hospital's comprehensive program. The individual program represents the micro aspect of planning.

The distinction between comprehensive and individual programs is quite important. When planning is discussed, one should realize that the macro aspect is more entangled and requires a myriad of inputs. The micro aspect is much more specific, and the task of planning is simplified by the narrowness of the activity. Determining the level of interest in a specific course offering is much less complicated than determining comprehensive interests for adult education. The material presented in this chapter is relevant to both types of programs, but it is especially directed toward planning comprehensive programs.

DEFINING PLANNING

Planning is a formalized procedure used to create programs. It is oriented toward the future and is the first step in creating programs. Some adult educators see the terms *program planning* and *program development* as being the same. Others (such as Rivera, Patino, and Brockett, 1982) view the terms as having different meanings. The primary distinction made between these two terms is that program development is a broader concept which includes planning as well as managing. In this book, no major distinctions are made. When planning occurs within the organizational context, very few distinctions can be drawn between planning and development.

Several other terms are worthy of special attention. One is *strategic planning*. For some, this term means long-range planning (beyond one or two years). More commonly, a strategic plan refers to proposed actions by which administrators systematically evaluate organizational opportunities and the potential impacts of environmental changes in an effort to fulfill the missions of the organization (Justis, Judd, and Stephens, 1985). In other words, it is a way in which an agency or company assesses needs, wants, interests, and the like, in society and prepares to offer programs which will address these issues and at the same time will help to fulfill the mission and goals of the agency or company.

A *master strategy* is a combination of strategic plans within a given institution. For example, a public school system may offer adult education as one of its functions. When the strategic plan for this program is combined with other plans for elementary education, secondary education, vocational education, and special education, a master strategy is created.

Progam planning provides the organization with numerous benefits. Among the more important are the following:

- It provides a master plan for the future.

- It ensures that adult education is not in conflict with the overall mission(s) of the parent organization.

- It provides the basis for formulating goals and objectives for adult education.

- It attempts to reduce potential conflict between adult education and other functions of the organization.

- It provides a guide for management decisions.

- It identifies critical components which should be infused into the development of programs.

- It increases the likelihood that all needs and desires receive appropriate review.

Boone (1985) identifies four distinct generic concepts which undergird planning.

- Planned change (aimed at producing certain outcomes)

- Linkage (establishes a relationship between adult education and other elements of the organization; between the organization and its environment; between the individual learner and the organization)

- Democracy (planning is best completed in a collaborative, participatory fashion)

- Translation (provides a document which clarifies objectives and translates environmental, organizational, or individual needs to objectives)

These concepts emphasize program importance. In their absence, planning is more likely to proceed in an aimless fashion.

APPROACHES TO PLANNING

Although various schema have been developed for program planning, no single system can be identified as being the best for all situations. This is true regardless of whether the organization is a public, nonprofit, service institution or a private, profit-motivated manufacturing company. Certain recurring common elements within the schema are recognized as essential components of planning. These factors are discussed later in this chapter. Essentially, approaches to program planning can be divided into two categories: nonintegrated approaches and systems analysis approaches. Nonintegrated approaches have been more prevalent in adult education. As organizations become increasingly sophisticated and as the knowledge base of adult education enlarges, greater interest is shown in systems analysis.

Nonintegrated Approaches

The one distinguishing facet of a nonintegrated approach to a planning process is isolation. The process is being carried out in a fashion which restricts participation and focus. Goals, procedures, and other relevant components are formulated for adult education without interfacing them with other divisions or functions of the parent organization. In addition, there is no conscious attempt to amalgamate the needs and values of the learners with the needs and values of the sponsoring organization or the environment (community, city, county, etc.). For example, assume that a church has decided to expand its operations into the field of adult education and establishes a committee to work with the minister to plan the programs. The committee focuses exclusively upon adult education programming. This approach often leads the planner to address the task by merely duplicating a program in existence elsewhere. This narrow vision of planning fails to consider how such programs may affect current or other planned functions of the church or how they relate to individual learner values and needs or interface with community values and needs. In reality, the creation of adult programs may draw resources from other programs, may compete for facilities, or may conflict with other initiatives of the church. These programs also may fail to address the highest priorities of the targeted population(s), and they may neglect to explore community factors which have a bearing upon the programs (such as other existing programs in the community and the basic needs of the community).

Some organizations can absorb the negative effects of nonintegrated planning without serious consequences. When problems arise, the flexible organization makes adjustments and resolves the conflict. In the case of the church, adjustments may be made rather easily to rectify unintended negative effects upon other programs. This can be accomplished if the church is a small and rather simple organization with a central authority who can make quick decisions. But assume that program conflict occurs in a more diversified organizational environment—one in which power is divided among a number of officials, factions, or corporate divisions. Adaptation is much more cumbersome because authority is dispersed in these situations. The use of nonintegrated approaches to planning usually carries a higher risk for more complex organizations. Often they must expend more energy to rectify the shortcomings of poor planning; not surprisingly, they are more careful that this function is completed properly.

Systems Analysis

As men and women have increased their knowledge of the world and themselves, they have exposed their ignorance. In other words, the more knowledge science has produced, the more scientists have realized how much remains unknown. This realization has inspired the evolvement of more sophisticated models for studying a wide range of problems, and it has resulted in more efficacious planning models for adult education.

Ludwig von Bertalonffy commonly is credited with the greatest contribution to the development of general systems theory (Laszlo, 1972). A scientist, Von Bertalanffy was concerned with life sciences, and he sought to develop systems theory for the organism, studying it as a whole and in relation to the environment. Eventually, he applied his work to other areas of study (such as psychology), and the generic attributes of his model soon were recognized.

A system is defined as a set of elements standing in relation among themselves and with the environment. It is based upon the premise that behavior and performance in organizations are the result of a unique combination of several components. Therefore, systems analysis becomes a way of viewing an existing whole by breaking it down into the its elements (for example, an organization is composed of many divisions and departments). The purpose of such dissection is to study the interactions and relationships of the parts to the whole and to each other in various combinations (Drake and Roe, 1986).

The use of a systems model for planning adult programs requires that certain data are available. Typically, these include the following:

- An accurate depiction of the organization as a "whole" (including philosophy and mission)
- Identification of the constituent elements of the organization
- Environmental restrictions upon the organization
- Internal (organizational and planning) restrictions
- Environmental needs and values
- Internal (organizational) needs and values
- Learner needs and values
- The mission and objectives for the program
- Identified outcomes

These pieces of information enable the administrator to plan using a sophisticated, integrated approach.

The systems approach reduces the margin for planning errors. It does so because it is holistic and analytical. Yet one should recognize that final planning decisions must be made by humans and, as such, are always subject to some measure of error regardless of the degree of sophistication (Banghart and Trull, 1973). For the most part, the use of systems analysis is predicated upon the theory that organizations are social systems (as described previously in chapter 5). Figure 7-1 illustrates how systems analysis is applied to adult education within the context of a parent organization. In this illustration, the environment refers to the external setting in which the organization functions. The planning process is one of simultaneously considering individual needs and values, environmental needs and values, and organizational needs and values and of doing so within the confines first of the environment, secondly of the organization, and finally of the planning process. Three basic elements must be developed for the systems approach: inputs, throughputs, and outputs.

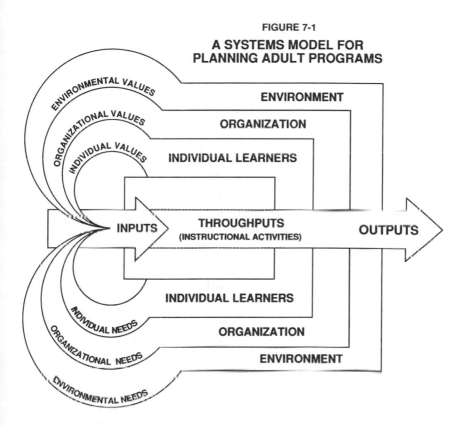

FIGURE 7-1

**A SYSTEMS MODEL FOR
PLANNING ADULT PROGRAMS**

Inputs are formulated using three pieces of information: the individual learner, the sponsoring organization, and the environment (Kowalski, 1983). These three sources provide the needs and values necessary for the appropriate design of programs. Inputs are established by converting needs to objectives. Needs and needs assessment will be discussed in greater detail in chapter 9. Examples of needs and values related to adult education are as follows:

Environmental needs:	Increase adult literacy.
	Reduce unemployment.
	Reduce mental illness.
	Increase civic awareness.
Environmental values:	Education is a lifelong process.
	Education should be accessible.
	Many agencies should provide programs.
	Education is a community commitment.

Organizational needs:	Increase productivity.
	Increase employee benefits.
	Obtain greater community visibility.
	Increase worker performance.
Organizational values:	Healthy workers are better workers.
	Serve all community members.
	Improve community life.
	Educated employees are efficient.
Individual needs:	Self-actualization.
	Increase knowledge in given area.
	More productive use of leisure time.
	Socialization.
Individual values:	Learning is important.
	Self-improvement is a high priority.
	Education makes one a better citizen.
	Education should be relevant.

Obviously, the values and needs presented here are merely examples. Some would be more prevalent in private industry, others more prevalent in social agencies. For example, a large manufacturing concern might have a need to increase productivity, whereas a community mental health agency may have a need to gain greater visibility.

Inputs included items such as books, teachers, and instructional equipment. Throughputs refer to the procedures which are conducted as part of the educational program. Instructional experiences are activities which are designed to bring about change in the learner (to change behavior or to improve performance). Outputs are the products of the educational experience and provide the basis for eventual program evaluations. Examples of outputs might be making adults computer literate, teaching an adult to read, or teaching an accountant a new system of data analysis.

Nonintegrated approaches to planning concentrate on the learning experience that is being formulated. Far too often, someone decides that a program should be offered, and little is done to validate the need or the impact upon the organization or the environment. Systems analysis urges the administrator to look simultaneously at the individual, the organization, and the environment. By doing so, the adult educator is less prone to ignore unintended by-products of creating new programs or modifying existing programs.

Systems analysis models of planning can be adapted to any type of organization (Murk and Galbraith, 1986). The model has become common in private industry and in large public service organizations. The use of a systems model to plan adult programs is enhanced if the parent organization already is accustomed to using similar procedures. In fact, well-developed institutions may insist that the adult education planner use such a model.

Linear Models for Planning

The most common method used to plan programs is a prescriptive technique which entails the use of a linear model. Linear models provide a sequential path that outlines the major steps to be followed in completing the planning task. Here the adult educator simply finds an outline in a textbook or borrows one from another administrator and religiously follows it in the planning process. This type of procedure is popular because it simplifies the task and provides a degree of perceived security for the planner. It is similar to the added confidence one possesses when one follows a trusted recipe in baking a cake. An example of a linear model is presented in figure 7-2. This illustration is not presented as an especially effective model; rather, it exhibits the sequential format common to linear models.

FIGURE 7-2

A LINEAR MODEL FOR PROGRAM PLANNING

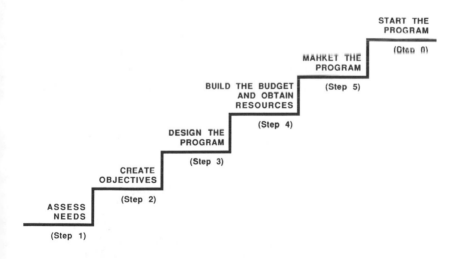

Linear models can be pursued in an integrated or nonintegrated fashion. Their primary value is that they provide logical paths to creating educational experiences. Their potency is devitalized, however, when they are used in a nonintegrated fashion. Regardless of how well each step articulates with the next, failure to plan in the environmental and organizational context is apt to breed problems. The use of linear models in a nonintegrated fashion is far less risky for planning individual programs. Since this task is less complicated, a number of models can be found in the literature for planning single programs (for example, Wagner, 1981).

Nonlinear Approaches

Some planners fail to use any model. This approach is analogous to trying to bake a cake by following your instincts. Obviously, if the cook is more experienced in baking cakes, previous exposure to the task enhances the chances of an acceptable end product. The same principle is true in planning adult programs. Experience can provide the administrator with some degree of craft knowledge. This information, accumulated largely by trial and error and the observations of others, allows the planner to make some effective decisions without following a specified format. But even for the most experienced, the probability for problems increases dramatically when one relies upon instinct, feelings, or hunches to make critical planning decisions. Leaving one ingredient out of a cake can result in an inedible product.

Not all nonlinear approaches could be termed as unstructured. Simply because a model is not linear does not mean that it is helter-skelter. Nonlinear models attempt to provide greater flexibility in terms of time and resource allocation. They avoid presenting lockstep avenues to creating educational experiences.

An example of one nonlinear model is illustrated in figure 7-3. As is evident, program evaluation is the central core of this model. The use of a nonlinear model is usually more difficult and requires greater resources—especially human resources. This is particularly true when several planning steps are being completed at the same time. For this reason, nonlinear models are not used as often as linear models. Advocates of this type of nonlinear model cite the following advantages:

1. The situation dictates which element will constitute the starting point for planning.

2. It does not assume that one must always go back to the initial step to recycle the planning process (Murk and Galbraith, 1986).

Both linear and nonlinear models can be successful frameworks for planning adult programs. A critical factor in selecting one over the other is an awareness of time parameters. Nonlinear models tend to require less time because components of the process may be completed simultaneously. On the

FIGURE 7-3

A NONLINEAR MODEL
FOR PROGRAM PLANNING

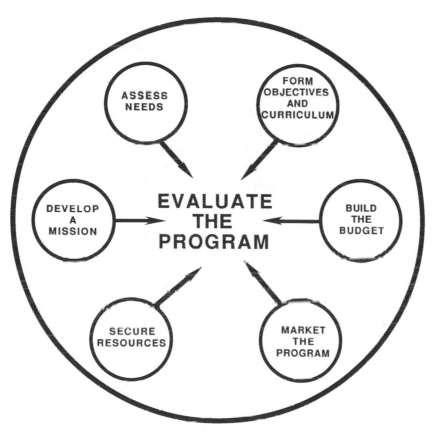

other hand, nonlinear models may require high-level planning skills and additional resources.

Prevailing Models in Adult Education

A number of authors have developed planning models for adult education programs. These schema exhibit substantial differences in complexity and in the degree to which certain values are expressed (such as efficiency and social awareness). Early models tended to be brief and concise. This tendency is exemplified in the five-step approach to planning created by London (1960):

1. Determine the needs of the constituents.

2. Enlist their participation in planning.

3. Formulate clear objectives.

4. Design a program plan.

5. Plan and carry out a system of evaluation. (p. 66)

The emphasis upon sequential, nonintegrated planning approaches remained common through the 1960s. Basic textbooks typically presented approaches similar to London's (for example, Bergevin, Morris, and Smith, 1963). Even today, there is little question that technical, linear approaches are the dominant force in program planning in adult education (Brookfield, 1986).

Gradually, adult education scholars are recognizing the problems caused by an emphasis upon simplicity—in other words, the restrictions of linear, noninteractive models. Houle (1972), for example, has devised a seven-step model which includes numerous subcategories in the critical areas of designing format and fitting this format into larger patterns of life. The social context issue has become a focal point of efforts in program planning since 1970. Many adult education scholars have accepted the notion that the failure to address the social, psychological, and technical variables affecting program planning was a serious defect in earlier models (Long, 1983). Accordingly, emphasis is shifting to interactive designs.

The interest in interactive models stems from two primary distinctions between this more complex approach and most linear efforts. First, planners recognize that the process of education is not value free. A multitude of biases, existing conditions, and similar variables serve to mold behaviors in organized learning. Second, interactive approaches are based upon the premise that certain planning tasks are pervasive: that is, they do not have identifiable beginning and ending points in the process (Simpson, 1982).

The most comprehensive analysis of planning efforts in adult education has been conducted by Sork and Buskey (1986). These researchers used the following evaluative dimensions to assess ninety-three publications containing some type of model:

- The sophistication necessary to use the model (the degree to which the planner needed special training)

- The theoretical framework (the degree to which the author provided convincing evidence to support the model)

- The comprehensiveness of steps in the planning process (the degree to which the steps were described and alternative formats suggested)

Their examination yielded several noteworthy results:

The investigators noted that there was little cross-referencing in developing planning models in adult education. In other words, authors tended to ignore the work of others and to create novel approaches.

There is a low level of theoretical explanation provided for planning models in adult education.

Few efforts have treated program planning in a comprehensive manner.

Most models vary more in contextual differences than in substantive differences: that is, most models presented are prescribed for a specific application (such as continuing education) rather than for adult education in general.

There is a heavy bias toward plans that use group interaction. Few models are addressing planning for programs intended for individual adult learners.

Most models ignore the specific roles and proficiencies required of adult educators in the planning process.

Although each of these findings is important, the second is particularly relevant to this book. In large measure, the gap in theoretical explanation can be attributed to a low level of emphasis upon the environmental and organizational contexts in which adult education occurs. No one model is suited for all situations.

CREATING A PLANNING CYCLE

Most sophisticated organizations no longer perceive planning as a finite process. Rather, they view this task as a continuing series of events which recycles itself at appropriate times. Research and craft knowledge indicate that certain procedures are critical to planning adult education programs. Although they are incorporated into a suggested model in this chapter, these procedures are the topics of most of the remaining chapters of this book. Thus, they will not be covered extensively here. Essentially, the planner can select one of four basic combinations with regard to a format:

- A nonintegrated linear model
- A nonintegrated nonlinear model

- An integrated nonlinear model

- An integrated linear model

Although circumstances should dictate which of these options is most appropriate in a given situation, integrated linear models usually are considered the best. These models provide a comprehensive view of the organization and the environment.

Condemnation of linear models, especially those which are basically technical adaptations of schema used in private industry, stem from concerns about the philosophical purposes of adult education. The primary attributes of these models, simplicity and efficiency, increase the likelihood that institutional objectives will dominate programming decisions. The formulation of program objectives, for example, tends to generate a narrow focus, a result which concerns some contemporary analysts of adult education programming (for example, Brookfield, 1986).

Nevertheless, an out-of-hand rejection of all linear models is myopic. Given the developing status of adult education, it is likely that many practitioners will continue to rely on less complicated pathways to program planning. The concerns which have been raised serve to increase the consciousness of practitioners to the potential pitfalls of using linear models in a restricted fashion.

Figure 7-4 provides a planning cycle for procedures which are recommended for planning adult education programs. This cycle is continuous in that evaluation of the program initiates the process once again. To ensure that this process is an integrated approach, one should use it in a systemic fashion (for example, as illustrated in figure 7-1). The very first step should be the establishment of the advisory council (or committee). This step occurs initially because the council becomes an invaluable source for information for most other planning steps that follow. Often, the value of an advisory council is perceived narrowly, and the council is used only to structure curriculum or to select instructional materials. Experience indicates that a well-balanced advisory council is a good sounding board for all planning activities.

One common error in planning is to ignore or to scan superficially the philosophy and mission(s) of the sponsoring organization. Having a clear perspective of how adult education will interface with the purpose of the parent organization can be critical. As already mentioned, these purposes can be dramatically different. Ensuring that someone from the parent organization is capable of making interpretations about philosophy and mission is important. Even more important is the strategy to involve this person in planning for adult education.

FIGURE 7-4

CRITICAL STEPS IN PLANNING ADULT PROGRAMS

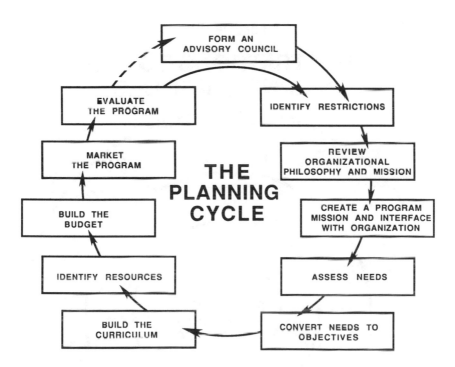

Advocating a linear model should not be construed as accepting past practice in adult education. Linear models need not be simplistic. They need not sacrifice appropriate considerations for the sake of efficiency. They do provide a structure, and if used in an integrated fashion, they can overcome the debilities of past practices.

RESTRICTIONS TO PLANNING

The best models for planning will be attenuated by restrictions which are either not recognized or not controlled. For this reason, it is advisable to devote specific attention to identifying planning restrictions. Basically, the planning process can be constrained by factors in the environment, the organization, and the planning process. These constraints are illustrated in figure 7-5. The planning is the central procedure and is affected by the three structures that surround it. Usually, planning constraints are the easiest to identify, and the environmental ones are the most difficult and complex barriers.

FIGURE 7-5

RESTRICTIONS TO THE PLANNING PROCESS

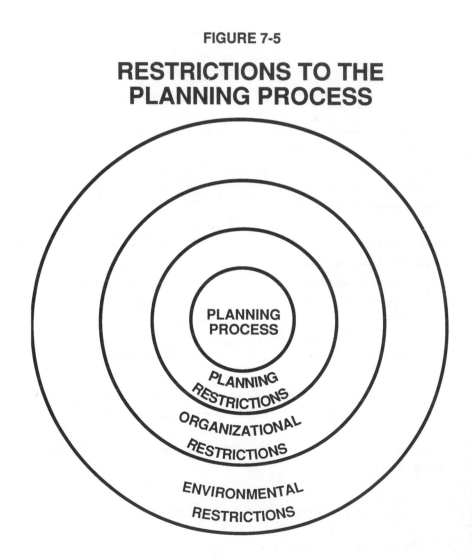

Environmental constraints refer to factors which exist outside the organization (such as barriers within the community). Examples of environmental constraints are a low value placed upon education, a lack of networking among potential providers of adult education, a great deal of competition among organizations for adult students, and a negative attitude toward lifelong learning. Organizational constraints could include restrictions such as a lack of commitment to adult education, a lack of monetary resources, inadequate facilities to conduct adult programs, a narrow vision of why adult education is valuable, and selfish motives for offering adult education. Finally, there are impediments related to the process of planning. They could include restrictions such as a lack of adequate funding allocated to complete planning, inadequate expertise by the planners, unrealistic time lines to complete the task, conflict among those doing the planning, and the use of simplistic models which fail to consider all relevant factors. Given the potentiality of these constraints to disrupt or restrict the products of planning, their identification should be a high priority at the very earliest levels of the planning process. In fact, this activity appropriately is considered a prerequisite to entering the planning cycle.

INVOLVING LEARNERS IN THE PLANNING PROCESS

Most adult educators accept the idea that program planning is enhanced significantly by involving the potential learners in planning activities. This principle has been reinforced periodically in the professional literature (for example, by Knowles, 1982). It stems from the beliefs that involvement creates a sense of ownership, helps build motivation, results in more relevant educational experiences, provides a democratic procedure which is valued by most adults, and even influences achievement. Unfortunately, the limited research that has been conducted in this area has failed to produce conclusive evidence of all these suggested benefits.

One recent study conducted by Rosenblum and Darkenwald (1983) examined whether adults who participated in planning achieved more than those who were not involved and whether adults who participated in planning ultimately were more satisfied with the resulting adult education experiences. Their study was conducted with a relatively small population (N = 28) of nursing supervisors. The results were negative in both instances. Those who participated in the planning failed to show higher achievement. Likewise, they did not exhibit greater satisfaction.

An older study conducted by McLoughlin (1971) found that participation in planning did not affect achievement but did make a difference with regard to attitudes about the learning experience: that is, those who participated in planning had better attitudes about the resulting adult education. Yet another study found significant differences in achievement and attitudes for learners involved in planning, but failed to exhibit differences in knowledge retention (Cole and Glass, 1977). One problem in analyzing such studies relates to the varying environments in which they are conducted. For example, different results produced from studies with mental patients and those with nurses may be more attributable to the personalities and experiences of the subjects than to the variables being examined.

Participation in planning has been shown to produce some desirable results in studies conducted in fields other than adult education. For example, a classic study designed to determine the effects of teacher participation in curriculum building in public school districts found that those who participate frequently exhibit a greater sense of commitment to the final product even though their participation did not produce a superior product, that is, superior to a product produced by a highly qualified specialist working in isolation. Studies which focus upon participation in planning suggest that such involvement will result in higher morale, maintenance of interest, and a willingness to change (Wiles, 1958). Select research results are fortified by craft knowledge, which leads many adult educators to believe that participation can be especially beneficial with regard to attitudes and ownership. The best-designed programs will have limited approval if people do not accept what has been developed.

The planner should be cautious, however, about making claims with regard to learner participation, especially where empirical evidence is either lacking or suggests that involvement makes no difference in outcomes. Private industry, in particular, is not overly prone to involve large numbers of employees in planning activities (as discussed in chapter 5). Thus, the adult educator is advised to examine carefully the intended outcomes before arriving at decisions about the participants in the planning process. Learner participation is fine as long as the planner can defend the purpose of that involvement.

A compelling argument can be made for learner involvement in what is termed "contextual factors." *Contexuality* refers to beliefs, moral codes, behaviors, and the like. Involvement in planning is more apt to result in the learners' awareness that their personal and social worlds can be altered by human effort (Brookfield, 1986). In other words, involvement raises consciousness and increases relevance. It also serves to create a balance in addressing the needs of the organization and the needs of the learner.

A decision to involve potential learners in program planning will rest largely with the circumstances that surround the planning activity. In certain situations, learners are more readily available and willing to become a part of the process. Even though it is difficult to provide strong evidence for some reasons related to learner participation, it is safe to conclude that this participation (if properly managed) will do no harm. Thus, in the absence of compelling reasons, learner participation should be encouraged.

SUMMARY

Adult education programs can be divided into two distinct categories: comprehensive programs and individual programs. The administrator may choose to use a nonintegrated approach to planning. Such efforts concentrate solely upon the program(s) being developed and ignore organizational and environmental factors. Increasingly, planners are turning away from nonintegrated approaches and adopting systems models for the critical task of designing learning experiences. Planning also can be viewed as linear or nonlinear. Often linear planning is condemned because it is not used in an integrated fashion.

There are elements of program planning in adult education which research and craft knowledge establish as critical. These include using an advisory council, assessing needs, formulating objectives, identifying resources, instructional planning, managerial considerations, and program evaluation. Successful planning requires the use of these critical elements within the contexts of environmental and organizational settings. Thus, the planner should not only understand planning theory and practice, but he or she should be able to interface this knowledge with information about organizational theory and practice.

Good planning is cyclical. It is not a process which can be ignored for prolonged periods of time. In that organizations always should be prepared to encounter the future, planning is viewed as a constant. Program evaluation concludes one cycle and provides the data to renew the process.

It is essential that the planner identify the constraints which will affect the process of creating adult learning experiences. These constraints can be found in the environment, in the organization, and in the planning process. Another critical factor which is especially relevant to adult education is the participation of learners in planning programs. Although there are positive aspects to this participation, the adult educator should exercise care in making claims about the value of this type of involvement.

FOR FURTHER DISCUSSIONS

1. Why are comprehensive programs more complex to develop than individual programs?

2. Identify some situations in which a nonintegrated approach to planning might be preferred.

3. Identify the differences between nonlinear and nonintegrated approaches to planning.

4. Some adult educators suggest that adult learners always should be involved in planning. Are there situations in which this may not be advisable?

5. In what ways do the missions and philosophy of the sponsoring organization serve to give direction to the planning process?

6. What is "craft knowledge"? Why is it beneficial to planning adult programs?

7. Why have linear models dominated practice in adult education?

REFERENCES

Banghart, F. W., and Trull, A. (1973). *Educational planning.* New York: Macmillan.

Bergevin, P., Morris, D., and Smith, R. M. (1963). *Adult education procedures: A handbook of tested patterns for effective participation.* New York: Seabury Press.

Boone, E. J. (1985). *Developing programs in adult education.* Englewood Cliffs, NJ: Prentice-Hall.

Brookfield, S. (1986). *Understanding and facilitating adult learning.* San Francisco: Jossey-Bass.

Cole, W. J., and Glass, J. C. (1977). The effect of adult student participation in program planning on achievement, retention, and attitude. *Adult Education, 27,* 75–88.

Drake, T. L., and Roe, W. H. (1986). *The principalship.* New York: Macmillan.

Houle, C. (1972). *The design of education.* San Francisco: Jossey-Bass.

Justis, R. T., Judd, R. J., and Stephens, D. B. (1985). *Strategic management and policy.* Englewood Cliffs, NJ: Prentice-Hall.

Knowles, M. C. (1982). *The modern practice of adult education.* Chicago: Association Press.

Kowalski, T. J. (1983). *Solving educational facility problems.* Muncie, IN: Accelerated Development Press.

Laszlo, E. (1972). *The relevance of general systems theory.* New York: George Braziller.

London, J. (1960). Program development in adult education. In M. Knowles (Ed.), *Handbook of adult education in the United States* (pp. 65–81). Chicago: Adult Education Association of the United States of America.

Long, H. (1983). *Adult and continuing education: Responding to change.* New York: Teachers College Press.

McLoughlin, D. (1971). Participation of the adult learner in program planning. *Adult Education, 22*(1), 30–35.

Murk, P. J., and Galbraith, M. W. (1986). Planning successful continuing education programs: A systems approach model. *Lifelong Learning, 9*(5), 21–23.

Rivera, W. M., Patino, H., and Brockett, R. G. (1982). Conceptual framework for program development. In C. Klevins (Ed.), *Material and methods in adult and continuing education* (pp. 99–105). Los Angeles: Klevens Publishing.

Rosenblum, S., and Darkenwald, G. G. (1983). Effects of adult learner participation in course planning on achievement and satisfaction. *Adult Education, 33*(3), 147–153.

Schroeder, W. L. (1970). Adult education defined and described. In R. M. Smith, G. F. Aker, and J. R. Kidd (Eds.), *Handbook of adult education* (pp. 25–43). New York: Macmillan.

Simpson, E. (1982). Program development: a model. In C. Klevins (Ed.) *Materials and methods in adult and continuing education* (pp. 92–98). Los Angeles: Klevens Publications.

Sork, T., and Buskey, J. (1986). A descriptive and evaluative analysis of program planning literature, 1950–1983. *Adult Education Quarterly, 36*(2), 86–96.

Wagner, G. (1981). Management steps in planning programs. *Lifelong Learning: The Adult Years, 5*(2), 10–11, 30.

Wiles, K. (1958). Does faculty participation produce curriculum improvement? *Educational Leadership, 15,* 347–350.

CHAPTER 8

Advisory Councils

Advisory councils or committees (in this book no distinction is made between the two terms) have become a standard feature of most adult education programs. This is true in part because some legislation which provides funding for select programs requires that these bodies be formed. In other situations they are manifestations of management's interest in gaining programmatic input. Increasingly, educators are recognizing two issues related to advisory groups in adult education:

1. Advisory councils have not been used to their fullest potential.

2. Advisory councils are critical to good program development.

Four specific questions related to advisory councils are considered in this chapter. First, what is an advisory council? Second, what is its rationale? Third, what are the major functions of this body? And fourth, what are the steps to creating and activating this committee?

DEFINING ADVISORY COUNCILS

The term *advisory council* has many meanings. It is difficult to pinpoint any single definition which would describe all such groups. Advisory bodies exist in a myriad of settings, but they are most common in public, service-oriented institutions. A definition becomes more meaningful when the discussion of this topic is restricted to adult education. In this book, the following definition is used:

> The advisory committee is a group composed of individuals who have knowledge and experiences which will be beneficial to the adult education

program. Many of these persons will not be educators; rather, they are individuals who by their occupations, common needs, or personal experiences can contribute to the overall process of program development.

Advisory councils may exist at three different levels. First, they can be formulated to provide input at the organizational level. For example, a YWCA may have such a group that is active in all phases of the organization. Thus, they provide the chief administrative officer with advice on many functions. Advisory councils also may be formed at the departmental level: that is, they may be designed to provide input for a major division of the organization. For example, the YWCA may have an advisory group for all operations related to adult education. Finally, there may exist program advisory groups. These bodies have the narrowest focus, concentrating on a single activity of the organization. An advisory committee for computer instruction at the YWCA would exemplify this level. In organizations in which all three levels of advisory groups exist, coordination can be a critical problem. Administrative direction is required to avoid conflicts between and among such groups.

A RATIONALE FOR ADVISORY COUNCILS

In education, the initial use of advisory committees can be traced to the development of vocational education. Professionals in this field recognized the need to create close working relationships with their counterparts in business, industry, and agriculture. They especially recognized that employers, employees, and community leaders were in a position to provide relevant information regarding program development (Cochran, Phelps, and Cochran, 1980). In this regard the advisory council not only supplied input, but also established a bond between the educational programs and those who were likely to be affected by the successes or failure of those programs.

Advisory councils also are congruent with the concept of democratic administration. Especially for public institutions, the notion that citizens should be highly involved in decision-making processes remains important. The use of advisory groups is one way of extending citizen participation beyond that of a policy board (such as a school board) (Salisbury, 1980).

Perceived and real gaps between education and occupational requirements became motivators for the use of advisory groups. Often leaders in industry would complain that the schools were not doing an adequate job of preparing individuals for the "real world" of work. The advisory committee became a communication vehicle to aid in the removal of these gaps. Such communication has dual benefits—the school learns more about job requirements, and the employers (and others) learn more about what is occurring in education. This interaction is more critical today than it ever has been. The rapid developments in science and its application —technology—require constant adjustments to educational experiences.

Persons who are a part of an organization often are unable to look objectively at the quantity or quality of their collective products. Vested interests, ego, and similar barriers frequently prevent these individuals from making unbiased decisions. It is not uncommon for divisions within an organization to oppose each other's initiatives simply because they want to protect power and resources. Without external input outside the organization, the real value of an activity may never be addressed. Thus, a school system may reject the expansion of an adult education program because the directors of elementary and secondary education argue that it will drain resources from their operations. An advisory council is capable of looking at issues beyond those of internal allocations and division of power within the organization. It can review needs and potential benefits to the community in a more global fashion. This type of review adds a dimension to decisions which can be productive both for program quality and for public relations.

FUNCTIONS OF ADVISORY COUNCILS

In adult education, advisory councils can serve a variety of roles and perform various functions. The actual expectations and activities will depend upon factors such as program scope, whether the sponsoring organization is public or private, the organizational climate of the sponsoring institution, the mission and objectives of the adult education program, individual needs, organizational needs, community needs, and the quantity and quality of human resources within the organization. In any event, there are certain services common to most advisory groups in adult education.

The first common function is *needs assessment*. Because the committee usually consists of persons with diversified backgrounds representative of the community, these individuals can be helpful in identifying what issues ought to be explored, the persons who should be contacted to complete the process, and what methods might be most effective in completing the task. It is not unusual for committee members to provide access to certain types of data which might otherwise be difficult to obtain. A personnel manager who is on the committee, for example, might gain permission for the adult education program to circulate a questionnaire in his company. A city council member may provide a mailing list from her office which will facilitate the assessment.

There are several areas in which advisory committees can become involved with *setting goals and objectives*. This task begins with a review of the organization's overall mission and objectives. Afterwards, councils can assist in formulating a mission and objectives specifically for the adult education program. Finally, they can interface these two documents to determine areas of conflict. Councils also may be used to set priorities in program planning. Often goals and objectives end up having a narrow focus. Advisory councils are one avenue for broadening input.

Advising on curricular content is another function which can be assumed by the advisory committee. As previously mentioned, the rapid development of technology has increased the value of this type of input. Seeking information from key individuals outside the organization obviously is more relevant for occupational programs, but it also provides valued advice for other forms of adult education, for example, recreational courses. Classes in adult basic education, for instance, could benefit from the contributions of experienced educators on the committee. These individuals may know of recently developed materials, equipment, or teaching methods that are relevant to the programs being developed.

Deciding upon an environment (for example, a classroom or laboratory setting) for the instruction is another critical planning decision. The advisory group can be a vital resource for *facilities decisions*. Because council members represent varied interests and experiences, their interactions regarding potential sites for instruction provide the administrator with useful ideas. They may know of available facilities, be able to cite problems encountered in the past, or offer views on desirable locations.

For some organizations, the *selection of qualified instructors* is a major task. The advisory council may be requested to generate suggestions regarding this aspect of program planning. Members of the council may know of potential instructors who possess the desired knowledge and skills. Their contacts with industry, the community, and social agencies increase the likelihood that an adequate list of potential teachers can be generated.

Many adult education programs rely upon their advisory councils to *assist with the process of recruiting students*. This activity is linked closely with needs assessment. Because of far-reaching activities in the community, individual council members may have information and insights regarding potential students. Frequently, council members are aware of the plans and directions of other organizations and agencies. Knowing that certain skills, knowledge, and experiences are or will be in demand in the community is an asset to effective recruiting.

In certain types of organizations, the advisory groups serve a purpose with regard to *community resource coordination.* The members know of other programs and services being offered in the community; using this information, they provide the sponsoring organization with recommendations regarding networking or similar concepts of resource coordination. This type of service is especially desirable in public organizations.

In private organizations, the advisory council may be called upon to assist with *professional development.* In some large corporations, the vast majority of what is termed "adult education" is related to staff development or human resource development. An analysis of work requirements, work habits, problems, and long-range planning is necessary for the council to make contributions in this area. Although this role for a council is more likely to exist in private corporations, larger public institutions often rely on advisory committees for input related to staff development. Advisory council members are prone to be sensitive to worker values, needs, and beliefs. As such, their input makes it likely that these factors will be considered along with organizational goals in planning staff development.

Every organization, regardless of type, is concerned with *public relations.* The advisory council can play a major role in this function. The mere involvement of a range of people in the community increases the likelihood that the adult education programs and the sponsoring organization will get more exposure. Persons on advisory panels often project a positive image of their activities with adult education because they usually perform this service out of conviction. The council provides a direct linkage between the organization's adult education efforts and the community.

Many adult education programs are concerned with *placing students in jobs.* This career orientation may focus on totally new employment as a result of completing a vocational course of study or a promotion within the organization after completing a specific learning experience. The advisory committee could be enlisted to assist with either of these goals. Vocationally oriented programs typically require an internship or similar work experience, and the council may assist with these types of placements as well (Riendeau, 1977).

The entire realm of *acquiring resources and building a budget* can benefit from input provided by an advisory council. Suggestions from members are not bound by biases existing within the organization. There may even be some members who have particular occupational or professional skills that are relevant to the courses being offered (for example, an accountant can provide ideas regarding resources for a course in bookkeeping).

One last potential function worth noting is *program evaluation.* This activity is especially meaningful for an advisory committee that has been highly involved in critical decisions related to formulating the program in the first place. Participation in program evaluation will provide council members with insights useful to all of their duties. If the group knows that they will participate ultimately in program assessment, for example, individual members are more apt to be deliberate in forming suggestions relative to planning. For instance, members will be more prone to set objectives which are meaningful to the learners. The council's interests should focus upon assisting with the structure of evaluation. Participation should not be interpreted to include the chores related to data collection.

Regardless of the scope of activities, it is critical to note that the basic role of an advisory committee is to provide counsel and recommendations—not to make final decisions. Weak organizations or weak administrators may lure such groups into making arduous administrative or policy decisions. Doing so constitutes an abuse of the persons who are volunteering their services. This lack of consideration could lead council members to resign when they realize they are being used to do someone else's job. Even if a council expresses a willingness to formulate policy, allowing it to do so is poor management. The council has no responsibility for the outcomes of such decisions. Experienced administrators know that a large part of making decisions is living with the consequences (Miller and Farrar, 1977).

CREATING AN ADVISORY COUNCIL

As the adult educator sets out to establish an advisory council, there are key steps meriting consideration. Although the level of the committee, the type of organization it serves, the scope of adult education programs, and similar variables will determine the best path to follow, the steps outlined here provide a general format that is applicable to the vast majority of situations. Nevertheless, it is important for the adult educator to recognize the uniqueness of each situation in which advisory groups are formed. Ignoring this fact makes it tempting merely to adopt what works elsewhere (Green, 1978). Differences among sponsoring organizations can be significant, and what works for one institution may not for another. Keeping this in mind, the recommended steps are presented in a preferred order.

Outlining Purposes. The first step in creating an advisory council should be the development of a rationale outlining purposes. This outline not only addresses broad purposes, but also lists responsibilities which will be assigned to the council. Organizing such groups simply because someone thinks it is a good idea or because it is expected in adult education is not solid planning.

To be effective, the council needs a purpose (Nance, 1976). Success often depends upon clear definitions of role, functions, and responsibilities which are understood by all parties concerned.

Structuring the Council. After the purposes and responsibilities are formulated, consideration shold be given to the structural elements of the council. These elements include the size of the council, the titles and functions of the officers, and the communication link between the council and the adult education program (that is, who will be the liaison person from the adult education program to the committee). Decisions need to be made about the length of terms for membership on the council and for holding offices. The size of the group will depend largely upon scope, purposes, and responsibilities. The group should be kept small enough to ensure that it is manageable and large enough to ensure that it can address the required tasks.

Gaining Organizational Approval. Before proceeding any further with the creation of the council, the adult educator should obtain the sanctions of the parent organization regarding the purposes, responsibilities, and structure of the proposed group. This approval will take different forms, depending upon the type of organization. In school districts, for example, the approval comes from a formal action of the school board, based upon the recommendation of the school superintendent. In private organizations, it most likely entails the approval of the chief executive officer or a designee. Regardless of organizational considerations, there should be an assurance that the sponsoring institution knows and approves of what is being done with regard to advisory groups.

Selecting the Members. Perhaps the most critical step to building a good advisory panel is the selection of members. Four specific criteria are suggested. First, the competence of individuals is important. What can an individual offer the council with regard to knowledge, skills, and experiences? Second, the level of interest in adult education (or specific program offerings in adult education) should be addressed. Since there are few extrinsic rewards for service on these groups, personal interest in the project is quite important. Third, the person's ability to devote an adequate amount of time should be assessed. Too often, important individuals are asked to serve, and their professional and social commitments do not allow them to participate at a very high level. Fourth, the character of the potential participants should be considered. Character here refers to the quality of a person doing more than just the minimum. Service on advisory panels often requires dedication and a willingness to do "extra" things. This character element can be explored by talking to persons who work with or have other contact with potential council members.

The use of criteria for selection becomes easier when formal standards for membership are established. These guidelines profile the desired attributes of prospective council members. They also identify who is responsible for recommending and approving council appointments. In a similar manner, standards are useful to prospective council members. They communicate the organization's expectations—information useful to one who is contemplating serving on an advisory council.

For most adult education programs, a broad base of representation is an important selection criterion. Especially in public institutions, this frequently means ensuring that the representation reflects the community to be served (Robbins, 1977). One asset of an advisory group is that it brings together individuals with varying backgrounds and experiences. If balanced representation is not considered properly, this advantage could be lost. Yet it is advisable to select individuals who share certain values that are pertinent to the tasks of the council (Wiles, Wiles, and Bondi, 1981). Selecting persons who hold vastly different values about adult education may result in inertia from an inability to agree on a philosophy and goals.

Finally, decisions relative to member selection should address the issue of how invitations to serve on the council will be made. Enlisting the support of prominent persons in the community will proceed better if it is done in a tactful and responsible manner. In some instances, such an invitation may be the first contact a prospective council member has with the organization. Therefore, care should be taken to perform this task with decorum. The level of formality depends again upon the individual situation. Even where personal contact is deemed important, it is judicious to issue a formal written invitation. If this invitation is extended by a high-ranking official in the organization, it is even more impressive and persuasive.

Orientation. Planning for an advisory council requires considerations for orienting the group to its purposes, responsibilities, and operational procedures. This process includes assembling a packet of written information which at the very least provides the following:

- A description of the sponsoring organization

- A description of adult education and the role it plays within the sponsoring organization

- A history of past organizational endeavors in adult education

- A statement outlining the purposes and responsibilities of the council

- Information about the structure of the council, including the number of members, officers, terms of office, and similar items

- Descriptions of existing and planned adult education programs in the organization

- A listing of human and major material resources for supporting adult education within the organization

- Role definitions for council members and officers

Plans also need to be made for orienting new board members in a personal way. These personal considerations entail introducing new council members to key persons within the organization, introducing persons already on the council, providing an opportunity to ask questions and receive answers, and giving verbal instructions which may not be available in written documents. It is especially crucial that new council members receive information about expectations. This may be in written form, but most often it is not. If the group is to be productive, each member must understand clearly what is expected and why (Wiles, Wiles, and Bondi, 1981). Far too often, administrators assume that everybody understands how councils function and neglect to instruct new members about ethics, policies, and similar guidelines. It is particularly important to interface the role of an individual member with the role of the committee.

Structuring Meetings. Often those who are invited to serve on advisory councils are professionals or executives who are concerned about the allocation of their time. They are accustomed to meetings which are well planned and executed. Neglect here can produce impatient members. One decision which needs to be made is how often the committee will meet. Frequency of meetings is in part determined by the prevailing expectations the organization has of the council. Far too often, the decision is made to meet once or twice a month with little or no thought given to whether this number of meetings is congruent with the tasks to be performed. An advisory council is apt to do two things if members find themselves meeting more than their planned role and function require. First, members may become disenchanted and fall into inactivity or even resignation. Second, the council may decide to create its own tasks, thereby increasing the probability of eventual conflict between the advisory group and the organization.

Other important decisions with regard to structuring meetings include deciding upon a time and location for meetings, a format for the meetings, and a format for agenda and minutes. The format can range from being quite formal, where rules of order are followed, to the meetings which are conducted in a casual manner. Regardless of the level of formality, it is sound practice to use an agenda and to prepare and approve written minutes of the meetings. These documents supply historical records which may be needed for practical administrative functions, evaluations, or future planning.

The adult educator may choose to allow the advisory group to make decisions cooperatively about structuring the meetings. In most situations, this method probably is preferred. It is democratic, and it allows the members to express personal constraints about meeting times. If this method is used, the administrator should be prepared to provide data which are pertinent to the task, for example, information on when facilities are available and when tasks must be completed.

Special Considerations. The vast majority of advisory councils in adult education serve without compensation. Administrators should keep this fact in mind. There are a number of courtesies that can be extended to the individual council members that reflect personal interest and a level of commitment by the organization. These considerations include seeing that the members receive parking passes and reimbursement for the expenses related to their service. They also could include scheduled activities designed to inform the members of the organization's goals and objectives, periodic lunch or dinner meetings paid for by the sponsoring organization, or planned ways of bringing recognition to those who serve on the council (such as news releases, awards).

The adult educators who work directly with advisory councils in large measure determine the ultimate value of such groups. If the council is viewed as a necessary evil, the committee is apt to be ineffective and there will be a low level of sensitivity to expressing appreciation for service. On the other hand, viewing the committee as a valuable asset should result in planned considerations that are designed to let council members know that their efforts truly are appreciated.

SUMMARY

Advisory councils are an integral part of planning adult education programs. They are vehicles for obtaining a broad base of input and for linking the adult education activities to the community. These councils may serve a myriad of roles and functions. Individual situations dictate the form and direction such groups will take. In any event, advisory groups should never be formed without a purpose.

A number of key decisions should be made in planning to create an advisory council. These include developing written documents with regard to purpose and functions, approving the process by the sponsoring organization, selecting committee members, providing orientation, structuring the meetings, and providing special considerations which express appreciation to the individuals who serve on the committee. Advisory groups can be quite beneficial, they can be a waste of time, or they can be a source of conflict. In large measure, outcome is determined by the perceptions of the adult educator who forms the council and the organization which sponsors it.

FOR FURTHER DISCUSSION

1. Why could it present a problem if advisory councils were allowed to determine their own role?

2. List ways in which an advisory council could be useful in coordinating community resources.

3. Would you rather work with an advisory council of five persons, ten persons, or fifteen persons? Defend your response.

4. Would private industry be more or less likely to use advisory councils for adult education activities?. Why?

5. In what ways would the sponsoring organization's climate affect decisions about the roles and functions of an advisory committee?

6. Should the chairperson for advisory committee be handpicked by the adult educator, or should the committee be allowed to select its own chair? Defend your responses.

REFERENCES

Cochran, L. H., Phelps, L. A., and Cochran, L. L. (1980). *Advisory committee in action.* Boston: Allyn and Bacon.

Green, L. (1978). Process before program: A recipe for community involvement. In M. M. Kaplan and J. W. Warden (Eds.), *Community education perspectives* (pp. 54–55). Midland, MI: Pendell Publishing.

Miller, B. P., and Farrar, R. (1977). Interfacing citizen participation with planning decision-making processes. *Educational Considerations, 4*(3), 34–36.

Nance, E. E. (1976). *The community council: Its organization and functions.* Midland, MI: Pendell Publishing.

Riendeau, A. J. (1977). *Advisory committees for occupational education.* New York: McGraw-Hill (Gregg Division).

Robbins, W. (1977). Utilization of community advisory councils. *Educational Considerations, 4*(3), 16–17.

Salisbury, R. H. (1980). *Citizen participation in the public schools.* Lexington, MA: Lexington Books.

Wiles, D. K., Wiles, J., and Bondi, J. (1981). *Practical politics for school administrators.* Boston: Allyn and Bacon.

CHAPTER 9

Needs Assessment

Although needs assessment is accepted universally as a critical element of adult education programming, a good bit of the professional literature continues to be devoted to detailing how this process can be effective and to encouraging practitioners to use it. The sustained emphasis suggests that this planning tool is not being used, or at least not being used effectively. The low level of usage can be traced to four primary factors. First, there appears to be a wide gap between theory and practice. Many adult educators fail to use this process as outlined in textbooks, preferring instead to plan programs on the basis of tradition, public relations appeal, intuition, faddism, political pressure, or the advantageous use of existing resources (Brackhaus, 1984). Second, a good number of practitioners simply do not know how to use needs assessment as a planning tool (Grabowski, 1982). Thus, they appear to be avoiding what they do not understand. Third, some adult educators see needs assessment as a luxury rather than as an essential segment of program planning. It is used when time, human resources, and fiscal resources permit. Finally, there are practitioners who view needs assessment as a potential source of conflict. As pointed out earlier in this book, many organizations perceive conflict to be dysfunctional; therefore, the process is disregarded. Needs assessment increases community exchanges with the organization, expanding the likelihood that problems will be identified.

The primary goal of identifying needs is to infuse the resulting information into the total process of program planning. Doing so results in more informed decisions on course content, course sequencing, and related instructional matters. Increasing the use of needs assessment practices is most likely when practitioners obtain a solid foundation of knowledge about this process, including a recognition of strengths and weaknesses. For these reasons, the foci of this chapter are definition, techniques, steps to implementation, and barriers.

DEFINING NEEDS ASSESSMENT

Sifting through the literature on needs and needs assessment can produce confusion. Ambiguity persists on this topic for a number of reasons, including the following: different terms are used by authors to refer to the same concept, identical terms are given different definitions, and wants and needs frequently are confused (Brackhaus, 1984). Adjectives commonly attached to the word *needs* add to the confusion. For example, *real needs, educational needs,* and *perceived needs* are used repeatedly in adult education; yet each has its own meaning.

Educational Needs. In its simplest form, a need can be viewed as the gap between what is and what is required. But there are different types of needs. For intance, basic human needs include requirements to eat and to sleep. These are needs that all humans possess. Educational needs are more diverse. An educational need is defined as the interspace between present behavior (competency) and desired behavior. Behavior may include cognitive growth, skill improvement, and changing attitudes.

Even though educational needs are relative to individual learners, organizations and communities also have needs. Educational needs stress learning and the changed behavior of individuals. Organizations and communities experience change by the modifications of their constituent members (individual learners). Thus, although the needs of communities and organizations may not be purely educational needs, often they are met by exposing constituent members to adult education.

Needs versus Wants. Wants usually are confused with needs. In reality, wants involve motivation—the individual's predisposition to improve. Alone, wants do not fully reflect needs. An individual may be incompetent in a skill, even one that is critical, but may not be inclined to remedy the incompetency. Primarily for this reason, a comprehensive assessment process ought to address both needs and wants (Scissons, 1982). Linking the two provides a data base which is more complete and more likely to produce the information needed for successful program planning.

Distinguishing between needs and wants becomes more difficult because of the different uses of the terms in professional literature. Knowles (1982), for example, views wants as the behavioral expression of needs and prefers to use the term *interests* to represent preferences or likings. In general, educational needs represent gaps between present competencies and desired competencies; educational wants describe an individual's predisposition to remove selected needs. Variations in the literature should not confuse this distinction.

Felt Needs. Felt needs are self-identified. They represent a conscious awareness by the learner of needs they desire to gratify (Monette, 1971). Alone, felt needs are not considered adequate measures for a comprehensive needs assessment. Nevertheless, they are a valuable component of the process. They provide the programmer with learner preceptions which, right or wrong, are an important element in programming. An example of a felt need can be observed in the person who desires to lose weight by learning more about good nutritional habits.

Some leading authorities (for example, Knowles, 1982) argue that felt needs are the most important type of need with regard to adult learners. This conclusion stems from the belief that felt needs are the strongest motivators urging persons actually to enroll in programs. There is little doubt that adults display greater independence in selecting educational activities. Therefore, a link with known felt needs ought to be productive.

Ascribed Needs. One way to determine needs is to have an observer detail discrepancies between the actual and desired behavior of others. This exercise identifies ascribed needs. Just as with felt needs, some degree of subjectivity is apt to attenuate the accuracy of the data. In particular, the values of the observer may play a critical role in distorting reality. Thus, although ascribed needs may be a contributing factor to a comprehensive assessment, used alone they are likely to generate insufficient information. An observer in a factory, for example, may determine that increased knowledge about the machinery being used will improve productivity. This determination may or may not be accurate. Insufficient information can lead observers to hasty judgments. But interfacing the observer's opinions with other information is more likely to identify the real needs: that is, assessing felt needs in addition to ascribed needs provides a way of checking one against the other. If the workers also indicate a lack of knowledge about the machinery as a problem, then the observer's conclusions are more credible.

Real Need. The gap existing between present performance and desired performance is referred to as a "real need." Real needs may be felt or ascribed, but not all felt or ascribed needs are necessarily real. Errors of perceptions and value judgments could make them inaccurate. Again, real needs are most often identified when multiple forms of input are used in the process.

Symptomatic Educational Needs. Although the common cold is caused by a virus, most persons associate the illness with its symptoms—a runny nose, fever, sore throat. Since no cure exists for the virus, relief is sought by treating the manifestations of the illness. Often, this same process of recognizing symptoms can be observed in adult needs. The individual perceives the manifestation(s) of an educational need as a real need. Take, for example, the functionally illiterate adult. He or she may never focus on the real needs (becoming literate); rather, attention is devoted to the manifestations of the need (not being able to be employed, social rejection). Thus, symptomatic educational needs are manifestations of a need which a person considers real (Bergevin, Morris, and Smith, 1963). Symptomatic needs are valuable in that they provide clues to identifying real needs.

Normative Needs. Monette (1977) uses the term *normative need* to describe the gap between a desirable standard and a standard that actually exists. Representing the distance between aspiration and reality, a normative need often is referred to as an *educational need* (Wlodkowski, 1985). Assume that the desirable standard for a typist is sixty words per minute with no errors. A typist who is performing at this accuracy level and producing fifty words per minute is exhibiting a normative need. Normative needs represent more than just what the individual wants to accomplish. They represent what is required or appropriate for a given situation. The educator, and not the learner, may be in the best position to identify a normative need.

Societal Needs. A society also may express needs. These needs might include increasing adult literacy, wiping out voter apathy, and reducing the welfare rolls. Most often societal needs are expressed at the community level, but they also may be manifested at the state or national level. Societal needs are aggregate needs. As such, they are common to a significant number of citizens. This number may or may not constitute a majority. Eradication of community needs through adult education is predicated upon linkages with individual learner needs.

Organizational Needs. Organizational needs are similar to societal needs but relate to an institution rather than to a community, state, or nation. Meeting organizational needs through adult education is accomplished by working with individual learners in a manner which produces the desired changes in behavior, skills, attitudes, and the like. For example, an organization may have a need to increase profits. Adult education is used to increase the human relations skills of salespersons in the hope that the organizational need will be satisfied.

Created Needs. When an adult has experiences which convert vague feelings into conscious needs, he or she is experiencing a created need. The experiences act as catalysts. Some needs exist below the level of consciousness; they may be in conflict with other needs. When these needs are aroused through structured experiences to a level at which the person reaches a decision to act, some adult educators refer to this need as a "created need." The term implies that the educator is purposely arranging experiences that are designed to allow this catharsis to occur.

Discrepancy and Derived Needs. One last categorization worth noting has been refined by Scissons (1982). In creating a typology of needs assessment definitions in adult education, he cites three potential components of a need— competence, relevance, and motivation. Competence refers to the ability to perform a range of skills; relevance refers to the usefulness of those skills in an individual's life or work situation; and motivation refers to one's predispostion to improve skills. Within this context, a discrepancy need exists when an individual's competency in a relevant skill is less than desirable. A derived need includes both a competence deficiency in a relevant skill and a predisposition on the part of the individual to satisfy this need.

NEEDS ASSESSMENT TECHNIQUES

Varying definitions point to one important conclusion—the programmer must exert care in determining the meanings of terms being used at any given time. Differences in the use of terms illuminate the inherent danger in using data collected by others (other agencies). Without carefully investigating the foundational constructs used in another's work, the programmer may make perceptual errors. Programmers (or assessors) may define needs differently, and generic applications of findings can be troublesome.

There are numerous tools that can be used to complete an assessment. In general, assessment practices are similar to evaluative practices. This is particularly true for the sources of input. In evaluation, it is considered good practice to obtain data from multiple sources. Performance evaluation, self-evaluation, peer evaluation, and supervisory evaluation collectively create a more comprehensive data base. Relying on just one form of input increases the probability of inaccurate conclusions. The same is true for needs assessment: using multiple forms of input reduces the probability of error.

Questionnaires. The most frequently used technique for assessing adult needs is the questionnaire, primarily because it is convenient. Questionnaires are relatively easy to administer and allow many persons to complete the task simultaneously without putting additional time demands upon the assessor. On the negative side, questionnaires are prone to error. The responder is unable to ask questions, seek clarifications, or interact with the assessor unless special provisions are made. The likelihood of error is reduced appreciably when the programmer heeds precautions to ensure that the instrument has reasonable levels of reliability and validity. Reliability pertains to the consistency of the instrument (that is, the questionnaire evokes the same responses from the same individuals in repeated applications). Validity pertains to the instrument's ability to generate the desired data (that is, the questionnaire measures what it is intended to measure) (Hopkins, 1976).

Questionnaires take many forms. Most typical is the checklist, in which the individual simply provides a response to an item by placing a check mark in a response column. Another common form of questionnaire is the Likert-type scale. Here the responder is asked to state his or her preference with regard to a given statement. For example, the statement might read, "I need to improve my reading skills." The learner is asked to give responses of strongly agree, agree, disagree, or strongly disagree with this statement. Some questionnaires use complex procedures such as Q-sorts (items are sorted into prearranged categories with set values) and Delphi techniques (responders rank a list of items, and then they rank this response and repeat the process until agreement is reached).

Questionnaires may either be open or closed. An open instrument allows the responder to use his or her own words in clarifying responses. By contrast, a closed instrument forces the responder to select from predetermined choices, but no provision is made for responder comments. Open instruments obviously produce more information, but they are more cumbersome to administer, score, and report.

Among the advantages to using the questionnaire are the following: it permits wide coverage of adult populations; it tends to be less expensive than other options; it may elicit more candid and objective replies when identification is not required; and it allows for consistency in the way questions are asked. The disadvantages worth noting include the following: the technique is impersonal; it frequently appeals to persons not skilled in data collection, who use it without knowing its limitations; closed instruments (which are more common) do not allow for qualifications of responses; and it is frequently administered without adequate tests for reliability and validity.

The most critical decision in choosing a questionnaire for needs assessment rests with its ability to solicit the desired information. The programmer must decide whether such an instrument is capable of serving the identified purpose. If not, a more precise instrument should be used. It does little good to select an instrument because of its convenience, only to find out later that it didn't produce the required information.

Interviews. The interview is similar in nature and purpose to the questionnaire. It involves direct interaction between the assessor and the assessee. Interviews may be conducted with a single individual or with a group. They may be structured with the content and procedures predetermined and held constant, or they may be unstructured—using a conversational approach. Structured approaches offer greater reliability.

Interviews allow the assessor to probe into responses—something not possible with most questionnaires. They also allow the assessee to ask questions. Skilled assessors are able to detect motivational factors through nonverbal behaviors, thereby generating additional data. The greatest debility of the interview is the reliance upon the judgments of the interviewer. Values and biases often condition the conclusions which are made. Interviews are also a time-consuming and expensive method of collecting data.

Job Analyses. In larger organizations, job analysis has become an accepted function within personnel administration. Analysis can occur in two ways. Reviewing written job expectations (job descriptions) is one method. Here, the assessor attempts to make an analysis by identifying job expectations which are no longer valid. The other method entails direct observations of work performance. The purpose here is to determine the discrepancies between present and desired levels of performance. Unlike questionnaires and interviews, job analysis data are generated by the assessor. Individuals who are being studied do not supply responses, and they are not asked to identify their felt needs. This is a limitation. Accordingly, job analysis becomes more powerful when it is conducted in a parallel manner to some form of self-analysis.

To the unskilled, observations may appear an easy way to collect data. In reality, good observations require high-level skills. For this reason, this technique should not be attempted by those who are untrained. Job analysis may be conducted in a structured manner, whereby specific behaviors are noted for quantity and quality, or they may be completed in an unstructured manner, whereby the assessor decides spontaneously what behaviors are noteworthy. One form of job analysis used in adult education needs assessment is the critical incident method. The basic premise is that needs can be exposed by identifying situations that characterize a given need as being present or not being present. Thus, a need is associated with a certain behavior; in this way, one can discriminate between those who have a particular need and those who do not. For example, good employees are deemed to be those persons who have good reading skills. This determination is used to generate a needs statement that all employees should be good readers.

Tests. Standardized or specially developed tests are used to collect needs data from adults. Written or oral tests may be used to assess skills, knowledge, or even attitudes. Standardized tests provide a good vehicle for collecting information, but certain examinations may not be effective devices for adult populations. Care should be taken to select appropriate tests. Many standardized tests are created for children (for example, intelligence tests), and using them with adults could result in improper conclusions.

Other Methods. There are several other techniques which can be used to collect data. Among the more notable are the following:

- Analysis of data collected by other agencies (health records, educational records)

- Needs identified by state or national surveys (census data, vital statistics)

- Scientific research (data in professional journals)

- Trend reports (studying common needs in similar organizations)

- Advisory committees (allowing committee members to identify needs through their own perceptions and contacts with the community or organization)

- Personnel records (assessing reasons for dismissals of employees)

Techniques for assessment are applied at one of three levels—the individual, the community, or the organization. A community survey, for example, may require the use of several techniques to accomplish its goals. The level of application refers to the scope of the assessment project. Typically, organizational and community assessments are more complex and require greater planning.

PROCEDURES IN EFFECTIVE ASSESSMENT

Although each organization should recognize the uniqueness of its task, there are general procedures for needs assessment which ought not be ignored. These elements provide a basic framework to assist the programmer with this complex task. The value of a framework is that it allows the process to be individualized. Ironically, some programmers reach an opposite conclusion. They think frameworks are recipes that provide universal principles that will be equally effective in all situations. This simply is not the case. The steps presented here should be manipulated to fit the situation confronting the programmer. They are intended to be a guide, not an inflexible set of mandatory linear steps.

Identifying Purpose. It is extremely difficult to design a needs assessment unless the express purpose for engaging in the activity is known. Purposes vary widely, depending upon the nature of the organization, the philosophy toward adult education, and so forth. Purpose gives direction to the programmer and the organization, and it also provides information for the assessee. For this reason, the purpose should be written in language which is readily understood by all parties.

The purpose of assessment may be singular and specific—identifying adult illiterates. It may be multifaceted—identifying educational, recreational, and occupational needs. It may be directed to identifying individual learner needs, organizational needs, community needs, or a combination thereof.

Determining the Scope. Another critical decision relates to the scope of the assessment (DiSilvestro, 1978). Who will be involved? Will it cover the entire community? In most instances, the organization will be targeting select populations. They may be employees of the organization; they may be unemployed adults; they may be housewives; or they could be an entire community population. Scope obviously affects many of the decisions in planning a needs assessment, but it is especially important for selecting techniques.

Determining Techniques. Since there are so many potential methods for collecting data, careful consideration needs to be given to factors which are most affected by such decisions. Cost, accessibility, time restraints, the nature of the information being studied, and the scope of the process are several such factors. Selecting techniques is one stage of planning where the services of a professional consultant may prove beneficial. This is especially true if the programmer has little or no experience with needs assessment techniques. What appears initially to be rather simple, can quickly evolve into an entangled procedure.

Determining Data Collection Methods. Simply selecting techniques does not resolve all concerns for data gathering. Some techniques require specified collection procedures, but others may not. Using a questionnaire, for example, necessitates additional decisions about distribution and collection. Cost and time elements are particularly critical issues for most needs assessments. The programmer may be forced to select less than ideal data collection methods because ample funding is not available or because certain time lines must be met. Since techniques and methods of collection are so allied, deliberations for these two procedures usually occur simultaneously.

Determining Methods of Analysis. Once data are collected, the programmer is faced with the task of sorting through the information. This task often entails much more than merely counting the responses. Some methods require sophisticated analysis (such as unstructured interviews). Not uncommonly, decisions related to analysis are ignored until data are actually collected. This point may be too late to discover that time lines cannot be met or that adequate resources are not available. By inserting this step into the initial planning phase, adjustments can be made either to the analysis process or to other aspects of the assessment, ensuring that analysis is completed in a congruent manner.

Raw data can be analyzed in several ways. For example, data could be placed in clusters using demographic information, or they could be applied directly to discrete needs (Grabowski, 1982). Clusters involve assigning results to groups which are established according to selected criteria (everyone over age fifty, persons who are high school graduates). Again, knowing how the analysis will occur before the assessment begins is an asset. It helps to clarify directions with regard to data collection.

Another aspect of this stage of planning is the provision for drawing priorities. Setting priorities from assessment results should be a standard practice. There are varying ways of completing this task. They range from simply assigning point values to responses to infusing organizational and community values into needs decisions. This latter procedure can be quite intricate. Typically, more complicated procedures require the adult educator to seek assistance from a specialist in assessment.

It is not feasible to detail all analysis procedures in this type of book. In addition to seeking assistance from a consultant, the practitioner can turn to the professional literature. A number of articles and books on needs assessment, some directed to adult education, focus upon data analysis.

Reporting the Findings. When should the planner determine the manner in which data are to be reported? This critical question is frequently ignored in assessment procedures. The decision of reporting techniques should be made early in the planning process. This increases the likelihood of appropriate data collection techniques, methods of analysis, and other relevant procedures for the types of information that are desired. Waiting until all data are analyzed before deciding how to report them can spawn at least two undesirable products. The final report may reflect only what is available and not what is really needed, or the report may be inappropriate for the primary audiences (for example, the report is so technical that the assessment cannot be understood by teachers, advisory committee members, and others). Having a perception of what the final report should look like early in planning can be a positive influence upon the entire assessment process.

Building a Schedule and a Budget. A time schedule is advisable for a number of reasons. Most importantly, it sets parameters for completing specific tasks and ensuring that the information being collected will be available when it is needed. A budget provides the fiscal boundaries for the assessment. Starting a project only to find that adequate funds are not available is frustrating and inefficient. Decisions regarding schedule and budget should be made before the process is put in motion. A schedule urges the programmer to recognize the uniqueness of each needs assessment activity.

BARRIERS

As previously mentioned, needs assessment is universally accepted, but not universally successful. In adult education, several barriers stand out as primary reasons for the process not being used or for its improper usage. Unfortunately, all of the attention to assessment activities in academic studies and the literature has not eradicated the problems.

Inadequate Preparation. A number of administrators of adult education feel inadequate with regard to needs assessment because neither their academic studies nor their experiences have prepared them for this responsibility. This inadequacy has two facets. First, many adult educators never received formal training in administration. They entered their positions without advanced degrees in either adult education or administration. Thus, they lack appropriate educational preparation for the task. Second, some of those who do have advanced degrees continue to feel inadequate because their educational experiences failed to provide sufficient exploration of needs assessment. This academic deficiency frequently results in adult educators attempting to conduct needs assessments with more creativity than knowledge (Brackhaus, 1984).

Poor Planning. Entering into an assessment without ample consideration for each step outlined in this chapter exposes the programmer to a high degree of risk. There are so many things that could go wrong. Despite this reality, some still choose to "play it by ear." Relying upon intuition to make progressive decisions once the process is initiated does not reflect the behavior of an educated leader. An effective programmer approaches the task systematically. A plan details each phase of needs assessment, individualizes general planning principles to the task at hand, and outlines what is to be accomplished at each phase.

Cost. Proper needs assessment relies upon multiple forms of data, objective data, and sophisticated analysis. This can be quite expensive. Many organizations either lack the resources or refuse to expend the resources to conduct the process properly. As a result, the programmer is urged to make do with what he or she is given. The rationalization is that a mediocre assessment is better than no assessment. In these instances, the cost of the process serves to block the programmer from doing an effective job.

Reliability and Validity Errors. In the discussion of techniques, both reliability and validity were defined. The most likely errors here are ones of omission. The administrator develops an instrument and just assumes that it is clearly understood and that it will generate the desired information. If wrong, the programmer is apt to accumulate erroneous data. Giving the organization improper information not only complicates the task at hand, but also reduces the credibility of the adult education enterprise within the organization. Top-level executives may become reluctant to fund needs assessments if they perceive the venture to be a worthless activity.

Analysis Errors. Improper analysis can reduce effectiveness in several ways. Needs assessment is a form of research, and the assessor should be skilled in data analysis. For example, not knowing the differences between nominal and ordinal data may result in faulty conclusions. In addition, setting priorities as a part of analysis is usually a cumbersome task. This is especially true when the administrator must integrate organizational objectives with the needs and wants of individual learners. Not infrequently, the adult educator attempts to complete these tasks even though adequate planning and resources are not present.

Political Considerations. Political considerations can be a barrier to the effective implementation of needs assessment in adult education (Brackhaus, 1984). This obstacle largely involves the use of values to interpret needs. It is possible, for example, for an assessment to produce needs which are incongruent with the goals of a community or an organization. Individuals may express interests in programs they do not need. Someone is forced to make decisions about these outcomes, and that someone usually is the adult educator. Fearing such potential conflict, the administrator may avoid assessment procedures altogether.

Monette (1979) points out that needs are not mere empirically determined facts; rather, they are complex judgments. Values are especially important when the educator is faced with choosing among conflicting or contradictory needs. The values of the client, the educator, and the culture affect the identification of needs. Value judgments are equally crucial when decisions must be made from a large list of needs (setting priorities) or when one needs to determine how identified needs will be met. In some situations, terms such as *right, good,* and *worthwhile* will assume importance in reaching decisions.

Contrasting Views of Assessment. Some critics (for example, Monette, 1979) argue that needs assessment is basically a normative function: that is, it is designed to measure the desired. Yet, much of needs assessment practice is concerned with measuring "what is." In doing so, administrators rely on technical approaches which emanate from scientific inquiry. But this inquiry cannot establish whether the desired is either good or right for the individual, the organization, or society.

Monette's criticism of needs assessment in adult education is quite relevant to the theme of this book. He views the suggested procedures as oriented toward predetermined objectives (that is, they are bureaucratic in nature, as described in chapter 5). Just as leaders disagree about how organizations should and do function, experts in adult education disagree upon the methods and purposes of needs assessment. The barrier of contrasting views is a most important issue. Knowing the variety of purposes that can be served by assessment and objectively interfacing this information with the specific goals of a project are the best ways to cope with this barrier.

SUMMARY

Although all adult educators support the notion of needs assessment as an element of programming, the concept has not been utilized fully. To some extent, differing definitions are responsible. Often, terms are used interchangeably, or different definitions are formulated for the same term.

There are many techniques which can be used to amass needs data. Decisions related to selecting methods are conditioned by the purpose and scope of the assessment. Knowing the advantages and disadvantages of the prevalent methods of data collection allows the programmer to make a more enlightened choice.

Even though each needs assessment is somewhat unique each time it is administered, there are critical steps which should be addressed in all situations. These include identifying a purpose, determining scope, determining techniques, determining methods for data collection and analysis, reporting procedures, and setting time parameters and a budget.

A number of barriers exist to prevent needs assessment from being utilized fully. Most are problems which can be resolved—inadequate funding and inadequate administrative training. The most critical barriers relate to value judgments and their potential for generating conflict. In many organizations, conflict is deemed unproductive; in these situations, adult educators are tempted to avoid the process.

FOR FURTHER DISCUSSION

1. List ways in which a needs assessment could be beneficial to the goals of an organization.

2. How would you establish reliability and validity for a questionnaire you developed?

3. Cite examples of how an individual's needs might conflict with an organization's needs.

4. What are the advantages of simply using an advisory council to establish needs? What are the disadvantages?

5. Why is it desirable to determine the method of reporting findings during the planning stage of assessment?

6. List ways in which an administrator could improve needs assessment skills.

7. List the differences between a Q-sort and a Delphi technique.

8. Identify a situation in which organizational values would affect decisions in needs assessment.

REFERENCES

Bergevin, P., Morris, D., and Smith, R. (1963) *Adult Education Procedures.* New York: Seabury Press.

Brackhaus, B. (1984). Needs assessment in adult education: Its problems and prospects. *Adult Education Quarterly, 34,* 233–239.

Castetter, W. B. (1981). *The personal function in educational administration.* New York: Macmillan.

DiSilvestro, F. (1978). Needs assessment and adult student services. *Lifelong Learning: The Adult Years, 1*(8), 4–6.

Grabowski, S. M. (1982). Approaching needs assessment. In C. Klevins (Ed.), *Materials and methods in adult education* (pp. 60–65). Los Angeles: Klevens Publications.

Hopkins, C. D. (1976). *Educational research.* Columbus, OH: Charles E. Merrill.

Knowles, M. S. (1982). *The modern practice of adult education.* Chicago: Association Press.

Monette, M. L. (1977). The concepts of educational needs: An analysis of selected literature. *Adult Education, 27,* 116–127.

———. (1979). Needs assessment: A critique of philosophical assumptions. *Adult Education, 29,* 83–95.

Scissons, E. H. (1982). A typology of needs assessment definitions in adult education. *Adult Education, 33,* 20–28.

Wlodkowski, R. J. (1985). *Enhancing adult motivation to learn.* San Francisco: Jossey-Bass.

CHAPTER **10**

Developing the Curriculum

W ho will be involved in the learning experience? What are the specific needs of the learners? What is the best way to organize experience to meet learner needs? What knowledge is of greatest value? These are but four of the many questions to be addressed by the curriculum development component of program planning in adult education. The very nucleus of a planned learning experience is the scope and sequence of content and learning experiences prepared for the students. Developing and coordinating these elements result in a product which separates organized adult education from spontaneous activities which are sometimes loosely defined as adult education. Curriculum development is therefore an indispensable subdivision of program planning.

Only selected aspects of a curriculum—those most essential to program planning—are addressed in this book. This is true for several reasons. First, most graduate students in adult education are required to take a separate course in curriculum. Thus, a more concentrated exposure to the topic is provided outside the realm of program planning. Second, the topic of curriculum is far too complex to be presented comprehensively in a single chapter. The material provided here presents a review of several key terms, a specific focus upon adult education, steps to building a curriculum, and a special emphasis upon program evaluation. Students and practitioners who lack a separate course in curriculum development are strongly encouraged to do additional reading on this topic.

PERCEPTIONS OF CURRICULUM

Not everyone views *curriculum* as having the same meaning. This is true in part because the term, much like *needs,* often is qualified by adjectives. Thus, a variety of definitions can be found in the professional literature. In this book, curriculum consists of all planned experiences that the adult learner receives as part of the educational program. Within this definition, *planned* means that the content of the curriculum is the product of analysis and purposeful structuring. *Experiences* refers to the entire range of activities the student may receive from reading a chapter, to writing a paper, to informally interacting with peers. Some authorities argue that *curriculum* and *instruction* are inseparable, and given the definition used in this book, that thought is acceptable. *Instruction* relates to the application of the curriculum and includes teaching practices, materials, tests, and the like.

Increasingly, curriculum specialists consider "all" planned activities as part of the curriculum. In adult education, it is not uncommon for the programmer to schedule a multitude of interactive functions designed to meet motivational, social, or similar needs. Although these activities may not relate directly to the subject matter of the course, they are part of the curriculum. Adult education is more likely to devote more attention to learning than to teaching (Knowles, 1982). This bias is reflected in the concern given to the real needs of adult learners. Planning focuses upon what is to be achieved (outputs) rather than on methodology.

Curriculum Theory versus Curriculum Development. Curriculum theory includes the study of what should be taught and how teaching should occur. The images and categories of curriculum presented later in this chapter exemplify theoretical considerations. Essentially, curriculum theory focuses upon what is (descriptive theory) or what should be (prescriptive theory). On the other hand, curriculum development concerns itself with the fundamental practices of molding a course of study. It entails deciding what to teach, learning experiences, and related planning decisions. Whereas theory involves study and reflection, development entails doing and decision making.

The Course Syllabus. Educators are often uncertain whether the term *curriculum* refers to a single course of study or to a group of courses. A curriculum usually relates to planning at the macro level. A series of five courses, for example, might constitute the certification program in continuing education for an accountant. Or one possible undergraduate major in college is the liberal arts curriculum. Deciding which courses should be included, the sequence of those courses, and the number of courses are components of macro curriculum planning. On the other hand, structuring an individual course of study is micro planning. The end result of planning a single course usually is called a "course syllabus." Syllabi give direction to teachers by presenting a listing of content and learning experiences. Both levels of planning, macro and micro, address the central issue of curriculum development—what should be taught?

Categories and Images. Various ways of categorizing a curriculum have been created in the past two decades. McNeil (1981) believes that all prevailing conceptions of a curriculum can be placed in one of four categories, as follows.

1. *Humanistic.* This orientation holds that the curriculum should provide personally satisfying experiences for each individual. This viewpoint has been a major factor in the thinking and prevailing practices in adult education. The influence of humanistic thinking is manifested in practices such as allowing adult learners to participate in shaping learning content and experiences.

2. *Social Reconstruction.* With social reconstruction, the emphasis is placed upon society rather than the individual learner. Improving society through education is the thrust of this category. Although social reconstruction has had some influence in adult education, the impact has been far less than influences which advocate the primacy of the individual learner. Advocacy for the belief that elementary and secondary schools should be used to bring about a new social order has received little support in the United States. Social reconstruction applied to adult education has focused more upon the quality of community life and adult life within the community.

3. *Technology.* Here, curriculum development is viewed as a technological process in which specified methods are embraced to insure that intended goals are met. Accountability is attained by achieving the specified objectives of the learning activity. The technological approach in adult education is most prevalent in large organizations which use education to further institutional goals. The administrator typically does not become concerned with the potential impacts upon society or the learner if those impacts are not specified in the program goals. As discussed in chapter 5, technical approaches are influenced by the desire for efficiency. Not surprisingly, these approaches become more common when demands for efficiency are increased.

4. *Academic.* This conception of the curriculum concentrates upon subject matter and broader fields of study. The learning encounter is supposed to provide essential knowledge and skills regardless of individual needs, societal needs, or organizational needs. This type of curriculum is prevalent in preadult education (elementary, secondary, and degree programs in higher education).

A slightly more extensive list of characterizations of the curriculum is presented by Schubert (1986). Noting that more than eleven hundred books have been written on this topic, he groups the various images into eight categories.

1. *Content or Subject Matter.* This is the most traditional image of a curriculum. It is somewhat analogous to the academic category already discussed. The purpose is to sequence courses and material within individual courses. The exclusive emphasis upon subjects to be taught ignores issues such

as cognitive development, creativity, and personal growth. This image of the curriculum is not effective in most adult education situations.

2. *Program of Planned Activities.* This image has a broader context than subject matter. Issues such as instructional techniques, motivational techniques, and a balance of subject matter are incorporated. Comprehensive curriculum guides are examples of this conception of curriculum. By insisting that the teacher rigorously follow only planned learning activities, this method often overlooks the importance of classroom dynamics. Although more relevant for adult education than the subject curriculum, this image does not provide ample consideration for individualized instruction. Social, psychological, and emotional needs may be overlooked in using a tightly prescribed instructional plan.

3. *Intended Learning Outcomes.* Here, a curriculum is perceived as the statement of what is expected from a learning experience. The emphasis is upon ends and not means. Designing an educational program is a process of selecting content and experiences that are likely to achieve the desired end products. This view of a curriculum does not recognize the myriad unintended outcomes of learning experiences. In adult education, there is a greater tendency for the students to exhibit a wide range of interests and needs than in the education of younger persons. Predetermined outcomes, therefore, are more likely to be restricting. Many benefits of engaging in adult education occur because the teacher is able to seize upon critical incidents and to be opportunistic in linking these incidents to learner needs and wants.

4. *Cultural Reproduction.* Some contend that the curriculum should be a reflection of society and culture. The community, state, or nation provides leadership in determining what should be transmitted to students. The values of culture become the focal point of education. This image is not very relevant to adult education. Adult learners are much more prone to criticize and question the material presented to them in an educational setting than are young learners. Their values are much more established.

5. *Experience.* This image rejects the notion that a curriculum should be a set of predetermined ends. Rather, the role of the teacher is to be a facilitator—to attend to individual needs reflectively. Means and ends are considered inseparable; as such, the curriculum is not fixed but evolving. This does not mean that subject matter is ignored; rather, subject matter is modified as circumstances and experiences dictate. The curriculum as experience is congruent with most principles of adult education. In fact, it is more likely to be successful with adults than with children. This is true because adults often are more capable of assuming responsibility and of determining direction for learning experiences. Educational settings which permit high levels of

individualization (for example, low teacher/pupil ratios) are especially conducive to this image of a curriculum. It also requires teachers who accept the notion that the learner is capable of selecting meaningful experiences.

6. *Discrete Tasks and Concepts.* This view of the curriculum is particularly relevant to training programs such as those in private industry or the military. A curriculum is perceived as a set of tasks to be mastered. It is assumed that mastery of those tasks ultimately leads to the achievement of a specified goal. For example, workers are taught to use a new machine by having them successfully complete a prescribed set of tasks (such as how to start the machine). Although this procedure is quite effective for mechanical skills, it is limited in other areas of education. Its use for certain forms of adult education may be quite appropriate.

7. *Social Reconstruction.* This view already has been described in McNeil's (1981) categories. Some adult educators see this concept as a means of improving community life, particularly for adult citizens.

8. *Currere.* Currere is the root verb form of *curriculum.* This image contends that a curriculum should be a reconceiving of one's perspective of life. It is a social process by which individual learners come to a greater understanding of themselves. The curriculum is the interpretation of lived experiences. This concept has some merit for certain areas of adult education even though it is pretty much rejected for preadult learning situations. Self-understanding is important to adults. This image of the curriculum can be found in some forms of adult education which stress improved mental health, self-actualization, and similar goals.

These categorizations and images should not be viewed as mutually exclusive choices. Rather, they provide a framework for the planner. Philosophical differences exist among adult educators as they do with any other group of professionals. These differences are traceable to the earliest books published in adult education (Sisco, 1985). Currently, there are those who advocate a focus upon life fulfillment (such as Stubblefield, 1981), human liberation (such as McGinnis, 1981), and social reconstruction (such as Healy, 1981). Knowing that course content and learning experiences are affected by the planner's perceptions is critical. Since adult education takes many forms, the image which is most relevant for a given situation is determined by variables such as general purpose, learner interests, learner needs, and organizational needs.

A FOCUS UPON AN ADULT EDUCATION CURRICULUM

The study of adult education has been influenced heavily by writers who have attempted to distance this process from traditional schooling (Griffin,

1983). In particular, the continued acceptance of Knowles's (1982) concept of andragogy has served to convince most adult educators that learner-centered approaches are absolutely essential. Partially for this reason, topics such as learner needs and learner involvement in planning have been given greater attention in adult education literature than has the process of curriculum development. There are several features of an adult education curriculum that merit special consideration.

Uniqueness of Adult Learners. Differences in the characteristics of adult and preadult learners are repeatedly stressed. These variations are deemed critical for adult education programmers and teachers. Practices and research reveal that not all popular beliefs regarding dissimilarities between preadult and adult students are valid. Adults appear to exhibit notable differences with regard to (a) motivation [higher], (b) physical speed [lower], (c) personality [more fixed behavior], (d) vision and hearing [regressive], (e) independence [more independent than children], and (f) expectations [desire self-directed learning, demand high levels of relevance]. Contrary to what many assume, they do not tend to exhibit differences with regard to intelligence (Kowalski, 1984). Learner characteristics bear upon philosophical and practical considerations in planning. In a country where education traditionally has been viewed as a youth-oriented activity, this is an indispensable reflection. With good intentions, some educators embraced practices considered successful in traditional schooling and applied them to adult education. Unknowingly, they violated sound practices for creating adult learning experiences.

Goals and Objectives. The design of a high school curriculum is governed by external factors (that is, external to the school) which restrict planning decisions. For example, state laws and regulations prescribe courses which must be taught or content areas for mandatory inclusion into courses. Other forms of parameters include minimum time requirements and college entrance standards. In adult education, there seems to be greater flexibility in curriculum planning. The range of learning experiences which fall under the label of adult education is much broader than in elementary schools, secondary schools, and even colleges and universities. Some aspects of adult education (such as adult basic education) may be more structured; however, in many other types of programs the planner is free to make comprehensive decisions about course content. For this reason, the task of interpreting identified needs into specific goals and objectives is critical to effective curriculum development in most adult education. These objectives allow enlightened decisions to be made regarding content, instructional methods, materials, and the like. Unfortunately, the program planner in adult education usually does not have access to standardized procedures to help structure the learning experiences.

Critical Considerations. Curriculum planning in adult education appears to be more open-ended than in traditional schooling. But appearances can be deceiving. An examination of critical variables which impinge upon planning decisions suggests that the programming of adult education may be less structured, but not necessarily less restricted. In general, there are five criteria which modify instructional planning. First, the planner is affected by philosophical considerations. The perceived value of learning, the image of a curriculum, and images of adult education exemplify philosophical considerations. These restrictions come from the programmer, others involved in planning, the organization, society, and so forth. Second, psychological criteria affect planning. This is especially true in adult education, where issues such as motivation and relevance are quite important (Wlodkowski, 1985). The various beliefs about needs and the nature of adult learners condition planning decisions. Third, issues of educational technology affect curriculum planning. Analyzing tasks, developing behavioral objectives, and using criterion-referenced tests to measure progress are examples of technical influences. Demands for accountability and efficiency are influential forces prompting administrators to initiate technical processes. Fourth, political issues modify the planning choices. For example, selecting activities and materials which are not discriminatory or offensive reflects political considerations. In larger organizations, political considerations may include gaining the approval of powerful executives. Finally, planning is affected by practicality. For many organizations engaged in adult education, this is a paramount issue. Included are restrictions such as program cost, required resources, and the organization's ability to conduct the program in a reasonable fashion (McNeil, 1981).

These restrictions point out that flexibility is not as great as some perceive. A number of forces converge to restrict decisions. Unlike planning for elementary and secondary schools, these restrictions are not always in the form of existing laws and regulations. The programmer is faced with the task of bringing the less formal restrictions to the surface so that they can be given ample consideration.

Cautions. Programmers in adult education often are tempted to borrow a curriculum from some other organization. Thus, a course designed for teaching auto mechanics at the tenth-grade level is adopted by a community college that is teaching the same course as part of a continuing education program for adults. The dangers of this type of adoption should be obvious. Psychological and philosophical criteria for a sixteen-year-old high school student may vary substantially from those for an adult learner. Even more disheartening, some administrators create programs with no prescribed curriculum. They simply allow the instructors to decide what will be taught, how it will be taught, and how evaluation will occur. The administrator assumes that the teacher is capable of making these critical decisions. Borrowing curricula and ignoring the need for structure increase the likelihood that the real needs of learners will not be met.

STEPS TO BUILDING THE CURRICULUM

Completing the curricular phase of program planning can be facilitated by using a sequential format. A step-by-step procedure is most beneficial, especially for programmers who have little or no experience or formal education in curriculum development. One such model is illustrated in figure 10-1. Identifying seven specific tasks, this linear model can be applied to virtually all programming situations. It should be noted, however, that simplicity has its price. Especially in adult education, where the values, needs, and wants of learners are so important, a linear model tempts the programmer to ignore vital inputs. The debilities of linear planning models were described in chapter 7.

The first component of planning is needs diagnosis. It is noteworthy that needs include not only those of the individual learner, but also organizational and societal needs as well. The next step, formulating objectives, is made possible when needs are analyzed properly and prioritized. Knowles (1982) identifies two types of objectives—operational and educational. Operational objectives identify improvements in organizational resources that are required for meeting educational objectives (such as increasing the adult education budget or making more classrooms available for adult education). Educational objectives describe the behavioral outcomes which are desired from the participants (students). These behavioral outcomes could include knowledge, understanding, attitudes, and the like. Objectives should be written and communicated to all parties who have a vested interest in the program.

Step three, selecting content, is based upon the objectives which have been formulated. For example, if an objective is to increase consumer awareness of the use of credit cards, the programmer must identify the sources of knowledge and experiences which allow this objective to be achieved. To some extent, the philosophy of the parent organization and the programmer affect decisions at this stage of planning. This is the area of curriculum planning in which adult education typically exhibits the greatest degree of variance from conventional schooling. This variance is due to higher levels of heterogeneity in student needs and fewer restrictions upon what must be included in the learning experience.

Several criteria should be considered in determining curricular content. One of these is *relevance*. Adapting content to the lives of adults is a critical

FIGURE 10-1

A PATH TO BUILDING A CURRICULUM

DETERMINE EVALUATION
PROCEDURE

ORGANIZE LEARNING
EXPERIENCES

SELECT LEARNING EXPERIENCES

ORGANIZE CONTENT

SELECT CONTENT

FORMULATE OBJECTIVES

DIAGNOSE NEEDS

process in designing learning programs. Relevance is measured by the degree to which the educational experiences relate to actual needs and problems. A second criterion is *teachability:* that is, can the material included in the plan be presented appropriately in the course, workshop, or other organized learning experience? *Flexibility* is a third factor to be considered. Adults typically exhibit a range of abilities, needs, experiences, and interests. Therefore, curriculum content should be flexible to allow adaptation to individual students.

Organizing the content, the next step, involves two key considerations. Vertical organization provides chronological order to the material, which allows instruction to be based upon a sequential pattern. Vertical patterns are usually formulated starting with the simple and moving to the complex or starting with the familiar and moving toward the unknown. In recent years, research has suggested that more sophisticated patterns for vertical organization may be used (for example, Posner and Strike, 1976). Horizontal organization, on the other hand, attempts to make the curriculum relevant to other learning activities, to life as an adult, to society, to work roles, or to similar considerations. With adults, horizontal organization of curricular content is extremely important. Motivational differences, in particular, require that learning content and experiences contain very high levels of relevance.

The presentation of prescribed content is an instructional procedure. Teaching involves the transmission of content through designed learning experiences. As an example, teaching a concept in mathematics could entail experiences with examples of the concept, nonexamples of the concept, independent practice, and group practice. Adult education usually requires that more attention be given to this phase of planning than would be true with children. Adults will expect classroom experiences to be more directly associated with their needs and interests and they are more apt to withdraw from experiences they deem unrelated to personal motivators.

Step five, selecting learning experiences, is a process identical to step three, selecting content. The formulated objectives serve as guides for determining which experiences will be incorporated into the program. As mentioned earlier, adult needs are likely to vary significantly; thus it is often necessary to highly individualize the planned experiences.

Likewise, the organization of experiences (step six) follows the process outlined for organizing content. Both vertical and horizontal factors are weighed in determining the sequence of experiences in the program. The horizontal considerations, those that link the learning activity to the life of the learner, are especially important in adult education. The instructor, for example, may decide to start with those experiences most related to the learner's personal needs.

The final task, selecting an evaluation procedure, is discussed in the following chapter. Keep in mind that this one path to building curriculum is by no means the only or best paradigm available. It is sequential and easier to comprehend than more complex nonlinear models.

COMMENTS ON CURRICULUM BUILDING

One debility of using a linear planning model is the tendency to view data in distinct categories. The needs and interests of adult learners, the needs and interest of society, the needs and interests of an organization, and subject matter content often intertwine. Step-by-step methods are more likely to ignore this reality. Rational approaches to curriculum development, much like rational approaches to running organizations (bureaucracy), emphasize objectivity and efficiency. Unfortunately, the real world is filled with barriers that make these goals difficult to achieve.

Building a curriculum is dependent upon having key pieces of information. Some contend that the order in which these pieces are considered is not that important (for example, Purvis, 1975). For example, it is possible to start with an evaluation procedure and to structure the learning experiences to fit it. The components listed in figure 10-1, therefore, need not be addressed sequentially—but they do need to be addressed. What follows is a brief discussion of several critical factors which mold the planning outcomes in curriculum.

Institutional Purpose

In elementary, secondary, and higher education, the mission and purposes of the institution play a major role in shaping curricula. A classic example of how this occurs can be found in the general studies portion of an undergraduate course of study. The motivation for colleges and universities to require such study is founded on a philosophical belief that the institution should produce well-rounded students. In adult education, the sponsoring organization also exerts an influence upon learning intent. Here, however, the influences may vary markedly. Elementary, secondary, and higher education are sponsored by schools. True, they may be private or public. But as institutions, they are all schools. Much of adult education is sponsored by nonschool institutions. This reality is important to curriculum building. In schools, the values which mold educational experiences are usually overtly stated. In nonschool institutions, the adult educator may be required to search for these values and expose them. The planner should not be lured into believing that organizational values are unimportant to curriculum planning just because they remain obscure.

Policies and Laws

Curriculum development also is affected by institutional policies and local, state, and national laws. Often state and national laws place parameters on adult education through connections to funding; that is, state and federal aid frequently have requirements regarding program compliance with certain standards. Examples of this control include a required number of instructional hours, requirements with regard to teacher qualifications, or class size restrictions. In the same manner, institutional policies often place restrictions on the planning process. This is especially true of personnel policies, which could mandate who could participate in adult education and under what conditions.

Values and Bias

Regardless of how detailed a paradigm may be, the influence of the planner cannot be totally eradicated (McNeil, 1981). Each adult educator brings values and biases to the process. In some instances, seasoned planners are able to deal with this influence openly. Take, for example, the issue of learner participation in planning. The adult educator may possess strong beliefs on this topic. Accordingly, these beliefs can influence decisions as the process takes shape. Planner values and bias may affect both process and substance.

A recurring concern throughout program planning is dissonance in values among the planner, the organization, and society. Where such discord exists, conflict is apt to be intense and pervasive. Determining the content and sequence of learning experiences is a process quite vulnerable to this problem. Whose values should dominate? Whose needs should dominate? The theme of this book is that there is no universally correct answer to these questions. A pragmatic approach synthesizing all values and biases is advisable.

SUMMARY

Curriculum development is a critical step in program planning. It can occur for a single course, producing a syllabus, or it can occur for entire range of programs, producing a master plan for all educational programs in the organization. In adult education, attention is increasingly being directed toward learning outcomes as opposed to teaching methods in planning educational programs. The uniqueness of the learner, varying goals and objectives, and a multitude of barriers make curriculum development in adult education especially challenging.

Although linear planning models have their faults, they do provide a reasonable pathway for the novice planner. More important than procedural steps is the assurance that all critical pieces of information are included in the process.

The adult educator often confronts the dilemma of considering diverse interests and needs. The individual, the organization, and society do not necessarily hold common beliefs or express common needs. Institutional purpose, policies and laws, and values and bias influence curriculum development from the earliest stages.

FOR FURTHER DISCUSSION

1. Explain why the human liberation perception is congruent with accepted principles of adult education.

2. Differentiate between curriculum development focusing on process and curriculum development focusing on outcomes.

3. Why would curriculum planning be a more homogeneous activity for elementary schools than it would be for private industry developing adult education programs?

4. Whose needs are stressed in the social reconstruction approach to curriculum planning.?

5. Identify two common problems with a step-by-step approach to curriculum planning.

6. Identify some ways that federal and state laws would influence curriculum development in public institutions and in private industry.

REFERENCES

Griffin, C. (1983). *Curriculum theory in adult and lifelong education*. New York: Nichols Publishing.

Healy, G. M. (1981). Adult educators should help citizens become involved in social reconstruction. In B. W. Krietlow and Associates (Eds.), *Examining controversies in adult education* (pp. 32–39). San Francisco: Jossey-Bass.

Knowles, M. C. (1982). *The modern practice of adult education*. Chicago: Association Press.

Kowalski, T. J. (1984). Research and assumptions in adult education: Implication for teacher preparation. *Journal of Teacher Education, 25,*8–11.

McGinnis, P. S. (1981). The focus should be on human liberation. In B. W. Krietlow and Associates (Eds.), *Examining controversies in adult education* (pp.24–39). San Francisco: Jossey-Bass.

McNeil, J. D. (1981). *Curriculum: A comprehensive introduction*. Boston: Little, Brown and Company.

Posner, G. J., and Strike, K. A. (1976). A categorization scheme for principles of sequencing content. *Review of Educational Research, 46,* 665–690.

Purvis, A. (1975). The thought fox and curriculum building. In J. Schafferzick and D. Hampson (Eds.), *Strategies for curriculum development* (p. 120). Berkeley, CA: McCutchan.

Schubert, W. H. (1986). *Curriculum: Perspective, paradigm, and possibility*. New York: Macmillan.

Sisco, B. (1985). From whence we came: A critical examination of selected historical literature of American adult education. *The proceedings of the 26th annual adult education research conference* (pp. 266–273). Tempe, AZ: Arizona State University.

Stubblefield, H. W. (1981). The focus should be on life fulfillment. In B. W. Krietlow and Associates (Eds.), *Examining controversies in adult education* (pp. 12–23). San Francisco: Jossey-Bass.

Wlodkowski, R. J. (1985). *Enhancing adult motivation to learn.* San Francisco: Jossey-Bass.

CHAPTER 11

Program Evaluation

Program evaluation has become an accepted part of program planning—at least in the literature. Practitioners are recognizing the value of determining successes and failures, not only for purposes of accountability, but for program improvement as well.

Most of us are prone to pass judgment on educational experiences we encounter. This is especially true in adult education, where learners demand greater relevance in curriculum and instruction. Personal assessments are valuable; however, they often are based upon a multitude of perceptions. Each individual makes evaluative decisions based upon self-constructed goals, values, and the like. Indeed, the root word in evaluation is *value* indicating that value judgments play an important role in the process (Fellenz, Conti, and Seaman, 1982). Too often, this one form of feedback constitutes the only source of assessment for evaluating programs. This chapter focuses upon program evaluation as a much broader concept. It is written in the belief that the characteristics of quality program evaluation are multifaceted, carefully constructed, and infused into the planning process as a primary vehicle for program improvement.

Organizations typically concentrate upon the performance evaluations of individuals. Far less effort is given to assessing the outcomes of total programs. Yet, both processes are temendously important to the well-being of an organization. The purpose of program evaluation in its simplest terms is to determine if a program is meeting its goals. Put another way, do measured outcomes for a given set of instructional inputs match the intended specified outcomes (Tuckman, 1985)?

UNDERSTANDING PROGRAM EVALUATION

Although there are many similarities between individual performance evaluation and program evaluation, there also are distinctive differences. These similarities and differences will emerge as definitions, purposes, and methods are explored. In this book, program evaluation is viewed as a critical, but often ignored, process in program planning. It serves two specific purposes in the realm of program planning. First, it helps tell the organization how well the program is working. Second, it provides insights into ways that the program can be improved (Simpson, 1982). Before examining these two attributes in greater detail, attention needs to be directed toward understanding the concept.

The Concept.

One of the most widely used definitions of evaluation is provided by Cronbach (1963), who views the process as the collection and use of information to make decisions about educational programs. This definition can include many facets of an instructional experience. There are two aspects of this definition worth noting: (1) the equal emphasis placed upon the collection and use of information, and (2) the purpose of making decisions. The collection and use of information is based upon the premise that sound evaluative decisions result from information (evidence) describing what actually occurred, not impressions or beliefs of what should have occurred (Wolf, 1979). In addition, an evaluative process is incomplete if it does not encompass ultimate decisions.

A similar definition of evaluation is provided by Cooley and Lohnes (1976): "An evaluation is a process by which relevant data are collected and transformed into information for decision making" (p. 3). The emphasis upon "process" is a key feature of this definition. If evaluation were viewed as a product, there logically would be a conclusion to the effort: that is, at some point the task would be completed. As a process, evaluation is never completely finished. It is ongoing, recycling itself as conditions dictate.

The two definitions presented here provide a solid framework for understanding program evaluation in adult education. In this book, the following principles are considered essential to quality evaluation:

> The collection of data is equally important as the use of the data.
>
> Decisions are based upon accurate and objective information of "what is," not "what should be."
>
> The task of evaluation is never complete without decisions being made.
>
> Program evaluation is a process rather than a product. It is never totally completed; rather, it is a continuous procedure.

Frequently, evaluation is confused with two other processes—measurement and research. Measurement is simply the act of measuring. It is a value-free procedure whereby data are collected using technical skills. In evaluation, quite the opposite occurs. Objectives of the program, which are the products of educational values, are the foci. Wolf (1979) contends that measurement and evaluation also differ in another regard. Measurement usually concentrates upon comparisons of results, for example, comparing the test results of two students. Wolf, and many others, view program evaluation as a noncomparative process. This conclusion is not necessarily true. In reality, program evaluation can be noncomparative or comparative. The real difference between measurement and evaluation lies in the area of values and judgments. Program evaluation entails two activities: measurement and appraisal. Appraisal is a subjective process in which the evaluator uses data obtained from measurement to determine if goals have been met (Houle, 1972).

Research is a process which is designed to generate new knowledge and to contribute to theory building (as described in chapter 4). Research results often are generalized to diverse environments, organizations, and the like. In evaluation, the focus is upon a single program. The processes are distinctively different; however, many of the skills required in one are necessary for the other. In fact, some authors (such as Cooley and Lohnes, 1976) use the term *evaluative research*.

Types of Program Evaluation

Most often, evaluation is dichotomized into two categories: formative evaluation and summative evaluation. Tuckman (1985) offers a third category he labels "ex post facto." Each of these should be understood.

The most widely used and commonly understood type of evaluation is summative. Scriven (1967) describes summative evaluation as a process designed to determine if a program should survive. Suppose that a company develops three different programs designed to increase the human relations skills of its middle managers. An evaluation procedure designed to determine which program should be continued after a trial period is a summative evaluation. In other words, the purpose is to collect documentation and to make a judgment as to which program is coming closest to accomplishing the goals. Uncertainty is a key element in summative evaluation. In this example, the company president is unsure about which course in human relations will make the greatest difference. He or she is willing to experiment—but the doubt generates the need for summative evaluation.

By contrast, formative evaluation concerns itself with improvements, not judgments. Using the example in the previous paragraph, assume a different posture by the company president. In this case the president firmly believes that learning experiences acquired though an organized program can increase human relations skills. Here the purpose of the program evaluation is not to determine if the program will continue or to compare alternative approaches; rather, the process seeks to identify ways in which experience can serve as a springboard to improving the selected program the next time it is offered.

The ex post facto process differs from formative and summative evaluation in that it is a longitudinal study. Using the same example of the workshop in human relations, assume that the purpose is to compare the results of a given workshop with the results reported in another company. Here the company is attempting to achieve the same results already reported by another company. The focus of evaluation is to compare the results of the program group with those of another group already tested. Because the other company has used the program and has reported its results, the comparison must be made after the fact, or ex post facto (Tuckman, 1985).

In summary, there are three types of program evaluation. Formative evaluation seeks to improve a program by identifying the degree to which objectives have been met and by using this information to adjust goals, procedures, and the like. It is noncomparative. Summative evaluation may or may not be comparative. It could be used to select one option from many or it could be used simply to determine if a program did or did not meet its goals. Ex post facto evaluation is comparative. It compares the results of a given program with the previous results of the same program.

Purposes of Evaluation

The express purposes of program evaluation are more varied than the types of evaluation. Fellenz, Conti, and Seaman (1982) identify seven such purposes:

1. To determine how well the program objectives are being achieved

2. To make decisions related to program improvement and future operation

3. To meet the requirements of the sponsoring organization

4. To provide feedback to the program participants

5. To describe the program outcomes to other educators

6. To become and remain accountable

7. To provide learning experiences for anyone interested in the program

Some of these purposes relate to the types of evaluation, and others are more general in nature. Clearly, the first and third purposes entail summative evaluation; the second and seventh relate to formative evaluation; and the fifth has implications for ex post facto evaluation. The fourth purpose focuses upon communication. Both students and employees can derive self-satisfaction and a sense of accomplishment if they are given program evaluation data. The sixth purpose is especially relevant to public organizations. Program evaluation offers a mechanism for providing patrons with an account of public funds.

Kinsey (1981) also developed a list of simplified purposes. Included are the following:

1. An evaluation may be designed to provide a descriptive analysis—a description of inputs, activities, or purposes of the participants and their involvement.

2. An evaluation may be designed to solicit reactions and opinions—of individuals and groups on qualitative and quantitative aspects.

3. An evaluation may be designed to identify and assess problems—the nature of problems, the importance of problems, and the causes of problems.

4. An evaluation may be designed to assess changes in knowledge, attitudes, and skills—the extent of changes and the relations of changes to goals and efforts.

5. An evaluation may be designed to assess behavioral changes—how clientele behave outside the program.

6. An evaluation may be designed to assess social impact—effects of the program upon the community or other collectives.

The relationship between purpose and type of assessment is critical. The reasons for completing a program evaluation should dictate the type of evaluation which is selected. Since organizations usually have more than one reason for doing a program evaluation, programmers are required to design an evaluative system which is eclectic: that is, a system which is both summative and formative, formative and ex post facto, or even all three.

THE PROCESS OF PROGRAM EVALUATION

For the practitioner, the actual procedures in conducting a program evaluation are most important. Adult educators want to know the "how to" elements. Unfortunately, it is not a simple matter of providing a recipe that will be successful in all situations. The process can be broken down into three components: (1) selection of methodology, (2) selection of participants, and (3) selection of a paradigm.

Varying Methods in Program Evaluation

Since evaluations are typically designed for individual programs, the methods employed may vary markedly. Three prime considerations affect methodology: (1) what criteria (standards) are to be evaluated; (2) how data will be collected; and (3) how data will be analyzed.

As previously mentioned, evaluation in its simplest terms deals with goal attainment. Since goals are influenced by values, the selection of criteria is an important element of the process. Take, for example, a class in computer literacy offered by a local service agency. The goals of this program may include any or all of the following:

To make a profit

To produce a positive attitude in adult learners toward computers

To increase proficiency in the use of a computer

To impart basic skills in computer literacy to participants

To enhance the image of the agency

To produce more effective learning results than were accomplished by the local public schools in offering the same course to adults

To produce a positive attitude in adult learners toward education

To increase the job skills of participants

To increase the critical thinking skills of participants

This list is not intended to be exhaustive; rather, it presents examples of goals often listed in program plans.

A range of decisions confronts the evaluator. Should general knowledge be measured? Should attitudes be measured? These questions focus on criteria for the evaluation and give direction to the methodology that will be used. Selecting criterion-referenced tests or norm-referenced tests, using questionnaires or interviews, using pretest or posttest formats, and using structured observations are but a few of the possibilities that the evaluator must ponder. An evaluation can employ a mixture of techniques. In complex programs, this is quite often the best strategy (Fellenz, Conti, and Seaman, 1982). Multiple forms of input are considered far superior to single sources in all types of evaluation. Relying solely on student evaluations of the instructor, for example, is more prone to error than a composite of student evaluations, supervisory evaluation, peer evaluation, and self-evaluation. For this reason, a number of authorities in evaluation and supervision recommend multiple techniques for collecting data (Goldhammer, Anderson, and Krajewski, 1980; Oliva, 1984).

Adult educators are often tempted to borrow program evaluation formats from other organizations. Faced with the demand to complete the task, this often appears to be an expedient decision. Two types of evaluation systems are available: (1) those created by an organization to serve a specific purpose, and (2) those created for large-scale use, usually commercially produced and marketed programs. If either option is selected, a number of caveats is in order. Given that models differ in type, purpose, and methodology and given that organizations differ markedly one from another, emulating successful evaluative practices is not an error-free choice. For example, most commercial packages for program evaluation in education have been designed for elementary and secondary school. Their use with adult programs may be inappropriate (Forest, 1976). The myriad of variables influencing the process creates a situation in which individually developed models are the safest option. Individualization is more likely to produce a methodology which directly addresses the needs and purposes of a given situation.

Selecting the Participants

Adult education literature contains many urgings that the learners should be highly involved in program evaluation activities (for example, Knowles, 1982). Although this recommendation is well founded, it often creates a sense of "tunnel vision" for the programmer; that is, the programmer concentrates on learner involvement and ignores the other potential participants. Involvement here pertains to planning and appraisal as well as data collection. In addition to the programmer and the learners, other potential contributors may be persons not actively involved in the program but affected by its outcomes (such as supervisors), adult educators from other organizations, organization employees not involved with the program (such as management staff from other divisions), members of a program advisory council, former students in the program, and consultants.

Again, the type of evaluation being conducted, the purposes of the evaluation, and the methodology being used are critical. Persons should be selected to participate for specific reasons. There should be an overt link between selection and purpose. Participants have a right to know why they are being involved and what is expected of them. If there is no link between participant selection and the structure and purposes of the process, persons are being engaged on the basis of the programmer's instincts.

Textbooks in adult education devote far more attention to the issue of planning participants than do books focusing upon program evaluation per se, partly for philosophical reasons: that is, principles of democratic decision making permeate most adult education literature. But this difference is also due to other perceived benefits. For example, learner participation can reduce the influence of the programmer's values in making appraisals of data (Fathy, 1980). This difference in attention to planning participants also occurs because many texts on program evaluation in education focus almost exclusively upon elementary and secondary education. As a result, planning and appraisal are viewed as tasks to be performed by "experts."

Building a Model

Good program evaluation is a cyclical process. The products of one cycle are used to refine goals for the next cycle. This is especially true if formative evaluation is being used. Earlier in this book, a caveat was issued with regard to using technical models for program planning. The same caution is valid with regard to program evaluation. There is no one recipe which will be effective in all situations. In fact, reliance upon a lockstep procedure can diminish flexibility to the extent that opportunities to expand measurement and appraisal are overlooked.

Figure 11-1 presents one model for conducting a program evaluation. It is a never-ending process consisting of ten distinct activities. Several phases in this model already have been discussed, for example, purpose, participation, and design. Others require mention here. Setting time parameters is one critical decision that must be made. Since the process is cyclical, there is a need to define the cycles, indicate when data are collected, indicate when data are analyzed, and so forth. To a large extent, the phases of this evaluation model are interdependent. For example, it is difficult to make decisions regarding data collection if time parameters have not been established.

A rather common problem in program evaluation relates to funding. The best-planned program will fail if adequate resources are not available to ensure that the components can be completed. Organizational officials who demand program evaluations should be willing to provide fiscal support to ensure that the task can be completed.

Data collection and analysis are primarily measurement activities. They could include gathering test scores, conducting interviews, or administering questionnaires. Evaluative decisions, on the other hand, entail appraisals. As mentioned earlier, appraisal is a subjective act. The adult educator, using the data base collected, determines whether or not specified goals have been met. This task is more complex than it appears. Suppose that a program goal was stated as follows: "Students should exhibit a marked increase in their attitudes toward engaging in an organized learning activity." The data collected reveal the following results from a standardized instrument administered at the beginning and end of a course:

- Ten percent of the students exhibited a much better attitude.
- Twenty-five percent of the students exhibited a slightly better attitude.

FIGURE 11-1

A MODEL FOR PROGRAM EVALUATION

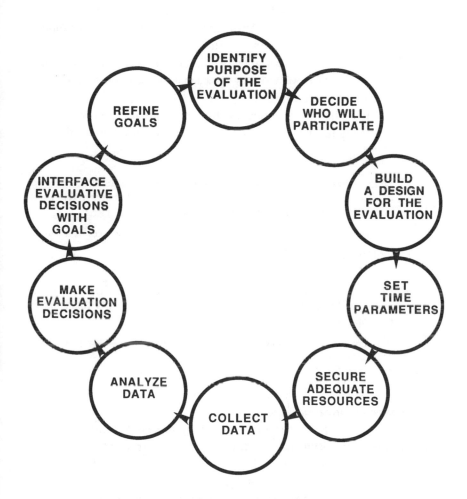

- Fifty-five percent exhibited no difference.

- Ten percent exhibited poorer attitudes.

Under these conditions, did the program achieve its goal? Five adult educators might answer this question in five different ways. The example points out the appraisal aspect of program evaluation.

This problem can be averted, in part, by requiring that all goals be specified in exact terms. Using the same goal stated previously, assume that the language is changed to read as follows: "At least one-half of the students will exhibit some increase in their attitude toward organized learning experiences." Is it easier to make an evaluative decision with this goal? Yes, because the goal is much more specific. Specificity, however, can be restrictive. Suppose that, once a course is started, unanticipated information suggests that some goals should be altered. A desire to alter goals once a course has started may be much more difficult if high levels of specificity were used to state the goals in the first place. Waiting until the course is over to change goals may not be in the best interests of the students or the organization.

The model in figure 11-1 represents but one alternative to constructing a program evaluation. In general, the following guidelines should influence decisions:

- Program evaluation should be individualized. The process should be directed toward the purposes of the educational experience. Differences in types and purposes affect the selection of methodology.

- Multiple forms of input are more effective than single sources of input.

- Evaluation entails both measurement and appraisal. Human and fiscal resources are needed for both.

- Learner participation is congruent with the values of democratic decision-making and reduces the likelihood that the programmer's values will dominate the appraisals.

- Program evaluation is a cyclical process. It never ends.

Reporting the Findings.

There are several good reasons that evaluation outcomes should be reported in some type of formal document. First, such a report communicates with employees and other participants in the learning process. Second, the report is an accountability document providing information to the organization and other possible sources of funding. Third, the report provides explanations for decisions which are made (Wolf, 1979).

Deciding when and how to issue evaluation reports ought to be addressed early in the planning process. Reports can be made on an interim basis, that is, as progress reports, or they can be made as a final report. In many situations, both may be required.

Long, cumbersome reports are at times unavoidable. In these situations, executive summaries are especially useful. Executive summaries are brief statements providing a minimum of supporting data and sketchy details of design and procedures. The focus is upon outcomes. The document is useful for reaching segments of the population that are not inclined to read the full report.

Tuckman (1985) suggests that the full report ought to include a minimum of two major sections. The first should cover methodology—such things as dates, site visits, interviewees, lists, and descriptions of observations. The second part should describe the evaluative decision—the conclusions that are reached. In reporting evaluative decisions, it is good practice to provide data that were used to reach conclusions, examples relevant to the matter, and statements explaining why certain decisions were made. Given the role of values in program evaluation, not all individuals are apt to react to conclusions in the same manner. For this reason alone, the inclusion of evidence is essential.

SUMMARY

Determining a system of evaluation is part of the program planning process in adult education. Consisting of two primary components, measurement and appraisal, the procedure allows the practitioners to make informed decisions regarding goal attainment. The three primary types of evaluation are formative, summative, and ex post facto. It is also important to recognize that evaluation can serve many purposes, from determining cognitive gains to assessing attitudinal changes.

There is no one best way to conduct a program evaluation. Individual circumstances dictate the model, methods, and instrumentation to be used. The procedure should be viewed as a cyclical process, allowing summative decisions to be made and providing data for program refinement. Properly completed, program evaluation provides feedback to the individuals engaged in the activity, informs the parent organization of outcomes, and serves as an accountability document for all funding sources.

FOR FURTHER DISCUSSION

1. Discuss the advantages and disadvantages of borrowing a program evaluation model developed in some other organization.

2. Discuss the ways in which personal values affect goals for programs in adult education.

3. Can a program evaluation be both summative and formative? Why or why not?

4. Assume you are planning a course in human relations skills for your company's employees. Under what conditions would you want to use an ex post facto evaluation to complete the task? What information would be required?

5. What are the advantages and disadvantages of stating program goals with a high degree of specificity?

6. List several disadvantages of relying solely upon students to complete an evaluation of an adult education program.

REFERENCES

Cooley, W. and Lohnes, P. (1976). *Evaluation research in education.* New York: John Wiley and Sons.

Cronbach, L. (1963). Course improvement through evaluation. *Teachers College Record,* 64, 672–683.

Fathy, S. (1980). The role an evaluator's values should play in program evaluation. *Adult Education, 30,* 166–172.

Fellenz, R., Conti, G., and Seaman, D. (1982). Evaluate: Student, staff, program. In C. Klevins (Ed.), *Materials and methods in adult and continuing education.* (pp. 335–345). Los Angeles: Klevens Publications.

Forest L. (1976). Program evaluation for reality. *Adult Education, 26,* 167–177.

Goldhammer, R., Anderson, R., and Krajewski, R. (1980). *Clinical supervision.* New York: Holt, Rinehart, and Winston (2nd Ed.).

Houle, C. (1972). *The design of education.* San Francisco: Jossey-Bass.

Kinsey, D. C. (1981). Participatory education in adult and nonformal education. *Adult Education, 31,* 155–168.

Knowles, M. (1982). *The modern practice of adult education.* Chicago: Association Press.

Oliva, P. (1984). *Supervision for today's schools.* New York: Longman.

Scriven, M. (1967). The methodology of evaluation. In R. Stahe (Ed.), *AERA monograph series on evaluation,* no. 1. Chicago: Rand McNally.

Simpson, E. (1982). Program development: A model. In C. Klevins (Ed.), *Materials and methods in adult and continuing education* (pp. 92–98). Los Angeles: Klevens Publications.

Tuckman, B. (1985). *Evaluating instructional programs.* Boston: Allyn and Bacon (2nd Ed.).

Wolf, R. (1979). *Evaluation in education.* New York: Praeger Publishers.

CHAPTER 12

Management Considerations

In recent years, scholars involved in the preparation of educational administrators have dichotomized management and leadership. The latter typically refers to supervisory functions entailing the specific application of professional knowledge, for example, supervision of instruction. Management, by contrast, relates to those functions common to all types of programs. These duties entail support services that must be performed, such as budgeting and personnel administration.

Distinctions between leadership and management have led some practitioners to conclude that one is more important than the other. In reality, both functions are critical to successful programming. Larger organizations usually can afford the luxury of employing several persons to administer adult education. In these instances, one administrator might be responsible for leadership functions (for example, a curriculum coordinator) while another might shepherd the management tasks (for example, a business manager). This division of responsibility and degree of specialization is not possible, however, for many providers of adult education. Smaller enterprises have a single person within the organization who is charged with the responsibility of total program administration. That person must perform both leadership and management duties.

Management encompasses a myriad of separate tasks. For example, fiscal management includes the preparation of budgets, cost analysis, resource allocation, budget administration, auditing, purchasing, and countless other tasks. The significance of management is recognized by most educators who prepare adult educators; as a result, students pursuing graduate degrees usually take a separate course in this area (separate from program planning). Three components of management are integral to programming in adult education and constitute the foci of this chapter. These are budgeting, personnel administration, and program marketing.

BUDGETING

Virtually all organizations, regardless of size and complexity, use budgets. A budget is a document outlining a plan of financial operations. Specifically, it sets forth an estimate of proposed expenditures for a given period or purpose and the proposed means of financing those expenditures. The budget is separated into categories called "budgetary accounts." These accounts reflect fiscal operations and conditions as they relate to the budgetary process. Examples of such accounts include estimated revenues, appropriations, and encumbrances.

Estimated revenues identify the amount of money expected as income during the life of the budget. In adult education, this could include money received from the parent organization to operate the program, tuition collected (if this money is put into the adult education budget rather than the organizational budget), donations, grants, and the like. Appropriations constitute authorization granted by the legislative body of the parent organization to make expenditures and to incur obligations for specific purposes. For example, an appropriation may be made for personnel which sets an aggregate limit for salaries. Another may be for supplies and equipment. Encumbrances are the commitments (obligated payments of salaries, purchase orders) chargeable to a specific appropriation. When these are actually paid, they cease to be encumbrances and are listed as liabilities.

Decentralized versus Centralized Budgets

The size and complexity of an organization obviously affect the budgeting process. Some organizations function with a centralized budgeting system whereby all divisions are subsumed under a single fiscal document. This method is efficient because there is only one large budget to prepare and administer. But this process has some major drawbacks. Little consideration is permitted for differing needs among various divisions. The tendency to treat all operations equally typically ignores special needs. For instance, adult education may require more staff development dollars than other divisions of the organization. In addition, a centralized budgeting system is administered by the organizational controller and not by the adult educator. This arrangement can reduce the authority of the educator to make decisions that have fiscal implications. This is a common problem in a good number of educational institutions. Educators often resent fiscal managers having control over their professional functions.

Decentralized budgeting allows each division of the organization to have its own fiscal plan. This process is more cumbersome, but there are attributes which may make the extra effort worthwhile. Decentralization usually requires a greater number of persons to become involved in the budgeting process than is true with centralized methods. This participation is likely to produce positive outcomes ranging from higher staff morale to improved decisionmaking. Moreover, decentralized budgets make it more probable that decisions affecting adult education are going to be made by those most closely associated with the program. Some degree of efficiency is, however, sacrificed with this procedure because larger numbers of persons are included in planning and administering the budget.

Developing a Budget

A budget is mandatory for sound program planning. The starting point for preparing this document is the educational plan which outlines the services to be provided. Budgeting in adult education can be conceptualized as an equilateral triangle with the educational plan as the base. The other two sides are the expenditure plan and the revenue plan (Candoli et al., 1977). This concept is illustrated in figure 12-1. If one of the sides of the triangle is reduced, the planner is forced to reduce the other two sides in proportion. A balance must be maintained among educational plans, expected revenues, and expected expenses.

The planner needs to devote special attention to factors which can have unusual impact upon operations. Special programs may entail unusually high costs; for example, a class for handicapped adults may cost more than other types of classes. Innovations also add to program costs. Pilot projects or creative teaching ventures might require equipment, materials, and the like which are not commonly used. Other factors of special note include staffing costs, salary adjustments (salary increases), operations and maintenance, fixed costs (social security, insurance), and supplies and equipment.

In a similar manner, the programmer needs to identify potential sources and amounts of revenues. Where will the money come from to operate the program? In adult education, the sources of revenues are largely determined by the nature of the organization sponsoring the activity. In private industry, most monies will come from internal allocations. In public schools, funds may be a mixture of grants, special state funds, federal funds, tuition, and local school district monies.

Approving the Budget

Preparing the budget is only the first step to formalizing the document. In most organizations, the budget needs to be presented to the persons having

FIGURE 12-1

COMPONENTS OF BUDGETING

EDUCATIONAL PLAN

the authority to grant formal approval. These may include high-ranking officials of the organization and the board of control. The presentation of the document can be extremely important. The programmer should be well prepared and exude confidence in discussing the proposed budget and anticipating questions. It is not difficult to detect when a budget has been assembled in a slipshod manner.

In most situations the budget must be formally adopted; even when this is not the case, it is advisable. This approval can be invaluable if fiscal problems are encountered. It is far better to have sanctions for the fiscal plan than to operate with uncertainty. If nothing else, the formal approval process facilitates communications.

Historically, budgets were considered to be rather mechanical functions: that is, the process was simply viewed as a method of fiscal control exercised by maintaining accurate figures regarding revenues and expenditures. Gradually, corporate executives began to view budgets as more than a necessary evil. Administrators realized that budgets could contribute to better management and leadership decisions. In recent years the use of budgets has evolved to an even higher level—one at which planning objectives can be measured in terms of resource allocation (Burrup, 1977).

The growing level of sophistication heightens the importance of formalizing the budget as a planning document. The success or failure of the program can be affected by the fiscal parameters established by the sponsoring organization. Progressive institutions recognize this fact and make available specialized assistance to the adult education programmer to ensure that the task is completed successfully.

PERSONNEL ADMINISTRATION

The full spectrum of personnel administration has many facets, including personnel selection, job classifications, record keeping, performance evaluation, and similar responsibilities. Within the process of program planning, five functions are most important. These are the structuring of positions, recruitment, selection, performance evaluation, and staff development.

Job Analysis

The programmer begins the functions of personnel administration by analyzing the quantity of positions required to execute the adult education programs. In general, positions can be classified as either instructional or support services. Support services include employees such as secretaries, custodians, teacher aides, and the like. The product of this effort is a listing of proposed positions accompanied by statements justifying the need for these positions.

Organizations typically follow a specified format for describing positions. These written documents are referred to as "job descriptions." The purposes of these statements are to identify accurately the nature of the position and the expectations of the position, and to list the qualifications required or desired.

Determining the number and types of positions needed is often more intricate than most practitioners realize. This is especially true when the programmer makes a deliberate attempt to create congruence between organizational structure and the use of human resources (Castetter, 1981)—that is, when the positions are carefully designed to fit within the existing climate of the organization. Assume that a highly structured and closed organization requires the services of a facilitator to conduct inservice programs. The nature of activities and the degrees of freedom for this position would be studied carefully to ensure that conflict would not be created once the person was employed. When planning is done at this higher level, the task necessitates much more than just guessing how many positions are needed.

Recruiting Personnel

A comprehensive plan for adult education includes information regarding the recruitment of needed personnel. This task may involve identifying internal resources (those already within the organization), but more often it addresses the task of finding needed personnel to enter the organization. Over the past two decades legislative acts have made recruitment and selection more prone to legal problems. Equal opportunity employment and affirmative action exemplify developments requiring the programmer to be more knowledgeable of personnel administration, existing laws, and corporate policies.

The structure of the recruitment program will affect the quantity and quality of applicants. For this reason, thought needs to be given to methods for recruiting as well as potential sources. Among the more common ways used to recruit personnel for adult education are the following:

- Newspaper advertisements
- University placement bulletins
- Mailings to select agencies
- Notices to public and private employment agencies
- Other media advertising (radio. television)
- Word of mouth

As with budget development, personnel recruitment may be a decentralized or centralized process. If it is centralized, much of the responsibility is shouldered by corporate specialists in personnel administration. Even so, the adult educator should have ample involvement to ensure that the organization seeks the right types of people.

Recruitment activities are governed by the policies which exist within the organization and local, state, and federal laws relating to employment practices. For example, nondiscrimination is a common recruitment and employment policy because of prevailing laws. In addition to such standard restrictions, an organization may have its own policies and regulations relating to issues such as pirating employees from other organizations or nepotism. Where they exist, collective bargaining agreements may present additional restrictions. Especially where personnel activity is highly decentralized, the programmer needs to meticulously review existing laws, policies, and regulations before establishing specific procedures.

Selecting Personnel

What types of documents will applicants be required to submit? How will applications be reviewed? Who will conduct the interviews?. These are but a few of the questions relevant to selecting and employing personnel. Recruitment and selection are not really distinctive processes; one flows into the other. Thus, comments regarding recruitment are valid for selection. Policy and legal restrictions and the level of centralization of the personnel function exemplify this fact.

Regardless of the size of the adult education program, the planner needs to establish a list of documents that are required to apply for a position. These typically include a letter of application, a resume, letters of reference, and placement office credentials (if applicable). Professional positions (teachers) usually require more detailed information.

The planner also needs to establish a procedure by which written material will be evaluated. Laws regulating discriminatory practices have moved many organizations to use objective and quantifiable methods to accomplish this task. Levine and Flory (1980) point out that the evaluation of written material is the most common selection technique—even more prevalent than the interview. This is true because far more candidates are eliminated at this stage than at the interviewing stage. Accordingly, most organizations have taken measures to ensure that written job applications are evaluated in a systematic and fair manner. Detailed records are maintained in the event that the organization is drawn into a legal conflict related to employment practices.

Interviewing is a critical step in employment. Regardless of whether the personnel function is centralized or decentralized, it is most likely that the adult educator will become involved in interviewing candidates. A practitioner who lacks training and experience in this responsibility would be wise to request inservice training from the organization's personnel office before assuming this responsibility. The job interview should be more than a mere discussion. It should be highly structured, serve specific purposes, and be justified in terms of the position which is being filled. The interviewer may be called upon (either by the organization or external regulating authorities) to defend criteria being used to make employment decisions.

Performance Evaluation

The chapter focusing upon curriculum development identified one form of evaluation, program evaluation. The other primary type is performance evaluation. Here the emphasis is upon the degree to which an individual employee meets the expectations of a position. Program evaluation is broader and investigates collective efforts and outcomes. Performance evaluation is more specific and is concerned with individuals.

Probably more professional literature has been devoted to the topic of performance assessment than to any other area of personnel administration. This is true for several reasons. First, it is a difficult responsibility for most practitioners. Second, it is a function which often creates conflict and litigation. For these reasons, administrators continue to request more information about the topic. Performance evaluation has become more sophisticated in recent years. In education, emphasis has shifted somewhat from assessing preexisting conditions (such as traits and skills believed to be correlated with effective teaching) to measurement-based systems which more accurately assess behavior in teaching and learning situations (Medley, Coker, and Soar, 1984). This shift is due, in part, to the greater likelihood that negative decisions made in evaluation could lead to litigation.

In general, experts in evaluation agree that multiple forms of input produce better and more accurate data. In planning adult programs, the administrator is encouraged to use several forms of assessment, including self-evaluation, student evaluation, peer evaluation, and supervisory evaluation. Performance evaluation is not a substitute for program evaluation; rather, it is another method for measuring goal attainment and making personnel decisions. This is another function that benefits from an official organizational sanction that identifies commitment to the process (Iwanicki, 1981).

Performance evaluation can serve two very different purposes. The first, and by far the most prevalent, is designed to identify employees who are performing below standard (summative evaluation). The second is much more complicated and relates to the development and professional growth of employees (formative evaluation). In recent years, experts have acknowledged the fact that both aspects deserve to be infused into a performance evaluation system (McGreal, 1983). Therefore, the system should be created to help people as well as to identify those who are performing below expectations.

Staff Development

The personnel aspect of program planning does not end with employment. Adult education is a field in which knowledge is expanding rapidly, and this expansion necessitates some form of inservice education to ensure that programs remain relevant. The degree to which such activities will be needed depends upon numerous factors, including the preparation of the employees to work with adults in an educational setting, the nature of the program offerings in relation to existing skills of staff members, the degree to which employees change (the frequency of employing new persons), the conditions in which the educational experience must take place, and the nature of the learners. Staff development is more likely to occur when time is devoted at the planning stage to formulate these activities. Otherwise, the commitment and funds are not available to execute the program. A sound staff development program allows employees to grow professionally as part of their employment (Campbell, Bridges, and Nystrand, 1977). There is a natural link between staff development and the formative aspects of performance evaluation. Staff development becomes the vehicle that helps teachers to improve. Enlightened organizations have abandoned the idea of using one day a year to engage in staff development. Rather, they inject the activities into ongoing operations.

MARKETING PROGRAMS

A third management function meriting focused attention in the planning process is program marketing. Marketing is the management function that is desgined to create an interchange between the organization and the markets and publics which could be served. Kotler (1975) has identified seven characteristics of marketing:

1. Marketing is a managerial function which also can be viewed as a social function (for example, material needs of society are identified and served).

2. Marketing manifests itself in carefully developed plans and programs.

3. Marketing seeks to bring about voluntary exchanges of values (it is a philosophical alternative to force).

4. Marketing entails the selection of target audiences.

5. Marketing is designed to achieve organizational objectives.

6. Effective marketing is user oriented (not seller oriented).

7. Effective marketing uses a combination of techniques (such as product design, communication, and distribution).

These characteristics provide a broad definition of marketing—one in which the organization relies upon exchange mechanisms to provide services.

Marketing has not been used widely within the profession of education. This is especially true in elementary and secondary education, where public schools enjoy a virtual monopoly. In recent years, colleges and universities have turned to marketing techniques to compete for a dwindling pool of students. In like manner, the need for marketing in adult education depends largely upon competition. It also depends upon the philosophy and mission of the sponsoring organization.

Marketing requires the analysis of four factors. First, product decisions (that is, the courses and programs to be offered must be identifiable). Second, pricing decisions need to be considered (tuition, fees). Third, one must determine distribution by deciding where programs will be offered. And fourth, communication and promotion decisions identify how contacts with potential users will be made (Smith, 1980).

Some (such as Dolich, 1981) consider the concentration upon pricing, promotion, and delivery to be too narrow an approach for marketing adult education. Referred to as "micromarketing," this restricted path is concerned with managing the organization. Macromarketing, by contrast, is a broader concept which not only illuminates the needs and successes of the organization but also the needs and successes of the society in which the organization functions. Marketing is evaluated according to its success in bringing about desired social change.

The distinction between micro- and macromarketing is quite important. If the desire is simply to fill the seats in a given course, the micro approach could be successful. If, on the other hand, marketing is designed to assist in bringing about social or other desired change, the organization is concerned with filling those seats with certain types of adult learners. Under these circumstances, macromarketing is more desirable. To be effective in macromarketing, the program must reach individuals whose behavior, skills, and attitudes need to be altered in order to obtain the results desired.

Promotion and marketing are not synonomous. Promotion is only one part of marketing. It requires the use of media and other communications to reach potential users (Shipp, 1981). An analysis of research studies reveals that consumers rarely rely upon a single source for marketing information. Marketing information tends to be cumulative, infusing media contacts with interpersonal communication (Holmsberg-Wright, 1983). For this reason, adult educators are encouraged not to rely solely upon mass media to promote their programs. Personal contact with potential students is likely to heighten interest in programs and provides an excellent complement to media efforts.

The more common promotional alternatives for adult education include the following:

- Public service calendars printed in newspapers
- Organizational newsletters and announcements
- Paid ads in a newspaper
- Paid ads on television and radio
- Public service announcements on radio and television
- Communication exchanges between organizations and agencies
- Informational bulletins sent to select agencies (such as employment agencies)

Far too often, interpersonal communication is overlooked. Former students, for example, are a good source of promotional activities. Determining the proper mix of these alternatives is a task conditioned by the nature of the program, the marketing philosophy (micro or macro), resources, and similar factors.

In large measure, marketing must concern itself with demand: that is, the ability to achieve objectives regarding the product or service being publicized is affected by the demand for that product. Kotler (1975) was able to identify eight distinct types of demands:

1. Negative demand (most potential users dislike the product or service and may even pay a price to avoid it)
2. No demand (potential users are uninterested or indifferent)
3. Latent demand (a substantial number of potential users share a strong need for something that does not exist)
4. Faltering demand (demand has dropped and further decline is anticipated without intervention)
5. Irregular demand (demand fluctuates)
6. Full demand (the level of actual demand equals the level desired by the marketer)
7. Overfull demand (the actual demand exceeds the level at which the marketer is able to or is motivated to supply it)
8. Unwholesome demand (the demand exceeds a level deemed to be acceptable)

This last type, unwholesome demand, is not relevant to adult education because it refers to vice products such as pornography, alcohol, and the like. Market conditions determine the plan that will be used by the marketer. For this reason, it is critical that the planner is able to identify accurately the type of demand that exists for the adult education services and to formulate a marketing plan that is congruent with that information.

There is a practical side to marketing. Within this realm the programmer attempts to be innovative, audience oriented, and well organized. Time frames and deadlines are established. Materials which are developed are ethical, tactful, and in good taste (Farlow, 1979).

There is every reason to believe that an increasing number of organizations and agencies will enter the practice of adult education. As this occurs, competition for students is apt to intensify. Proven marketing methods can be borrowed from private industry, but such imitation is likely to ignore the social elements of adult education. For many public, service, nonprofit institutions, macromarketing is a more appropriate path to follow.

SUMMARY

Administration in adult education can be divided into those activities that involve leadership (such as instructional supervision) and those activities that address management (such as fiscal management). Three primary areas of management connected with program planning are budgeting, personnel, and marketing.

Budgets can be either centralized or decentralized, with the latter requiring more detailed attention. The formulation of the budget can be conceived as a triangle with three sides: an educational plan, an expenditure plan, and a revenue plan. Each affects the others. Since the budget is itself a planning document, formal approval is a critical step.

Personnel considerations in planning focus around five processes: job analysis, recruitment, selection, performance evaluation, and staff development. Increasingly, laws, policies, and regulations are making personnel functions more complex and prone to litigation.

Marketing is a method of exchange in which an organization or agency attempts to provide a product or service. In doing so, the planner must be able to identify the market conditions that exist. In addition, a mix of communication avenues, including interpersonal contacts, needs to be devised. Unlike private industry, which may concentrate on selling its product, social agencies ought to concern themselves with the outcomes of the services they are attempting to market.

FOR FURTHER DISCUSSION

1. Discuss the problems that would be encountered if a formal budget did not exist for an adult education program.

2. Defend decentralized budgeting from the perspective of an educator. Defend centralized budgeting from the perspective of a manager.

3. Why are personnel administration decisions important to program planning?

4. Describe the difference between job analysis and job description.

5. In what ways does macromarketing address social objectives in adult education?

6. Is it better to devise a marketing plan after the program is planned? Why or why not?

7. Describe the difference between leadership and management.

REFERENCES

Burrup, P. E. (1977). *Financing education in a climate of change.* Boston: Allyn and Bacon.

Campbell, R. F., Bridges, E. M., and Nystrand, R. O. (1977). *Introduction to educational administration.* Boston: Allyn and Bacon.

Candoli, I. C., Hack, W. G., Ray, J. R., and Stollar, D. H. (1977). *School business administration: A planning approach.* Boston: Allyn and Bacon.

Castetter, W. B. (1981). *The personnel function in educational administration.* New York: Macmillan.

Dolich, P. L. (1981). A social marketing system approach in adult education. *Lifelong Learning: The Adult Years, 4*(5), 10–13.

Farlow, H. (1979). *Publicizing and promoting programs.* New York: McGraw-Hill.

Holmsberg-Wright, K. (1983). Promoting your adult education program: The use of interpersonal communication. *Lifelong Learning: The Adult Years, 6*(8), 4–5.

Iwanicki, E. (1981). Contract plans: A professional growth-oriented approach to evaluating teacher performance. In J. Millman (Ed.), *Handbook of teacher evaluation* (pp. 203–228). Beverly Hills, CA: Sage Publications.

Kotler, P. (1975). *Marketing for nonprofit organizations.* Englewood Cliffs, N. J.: Prentice-Hall.

Levine, E. L., and Flory, A. (1980). Evaluation of job applications—A conceptual framework. In M. J. Levine (Ed.), *Public personnel management* (pp. 15–24). Salt Lake City, UT: Brighton Publishing.

McGreal, T. L. (1983). *Successful teacher evaluation.* Alexandria, VA: Association for Supervision and Curriculum Development.

Medley, D. M., Coker, H., and Soar, R. S. (1984). *Measurement-based teacher evaluation.* New York: Longman.

Shipp, T. (1981). The marketing concept and adult education. *Lifelong Learning: The Adult Years, 4*(4), 8–9.

Smith, W. C. (1980). Marketing—a controllable tool for education administrators. *Lifelong Learning: The Adult Years, 4*(3), 8–10.

PART IV

The Future of Planning

CHAPTER 13

Adult Education: An Emerging Social Service

(This chapter was coauthored by John Fallon, Executive Assistant to the President, Saginaw Valley State College, Michigan.)

There are many forces operating to influence adult education development. Some can be considered the effects of the natural evolution of the society and occur with little deliberate planning or control. Others are interventions designed to mediate the effects of a rapidly changing society. Still others are products of the adult education profession itself, which has one foot in a past age of marginality and the other in an emerging age of critical importance. Directly or indirectly, all such forces are serving to clarify the missions of adult education; as such, they have implications for program planning. An understanding of this progression helps the program planner anticipate tomorrow's needs.

Several dimensions of change in adult education are especially note worthy in the realm of program planning. They include the following:

The nature of public perceptions of adult education

The concept of lifelong education (which is closely related to adult education semantically, practically, and theoretically)

Research and its importance in relation to the legitimacy of adult education

The need to integrate adult education into the central educational mission of organizations, institutions, agencies, and the like

Although the above list is by no means exhaustive, it serves to identify the more important factors refining adult education. John Dewey emphasized the critical nature of growth as an educational goal. In this regard, refinement reflects the improvements and growth of adult education as a field of study and as a social practice.

CHANGING PUBLIC PERCEPTIONS OF ADULT EDUCATION

There is little question that the beliefs and behaviors of the public toward education are important. In a field of social practice which depends largely on various forms of public involvement, it could be argued that the collective perception of the population is the single most significant issue. This view is based on the idea that human perception influences attitude and, ultimately, behavior. The nature of the public perception of adult education, therefore, potentially affects every dimension of practice. In large measure, this perception becomes a potent environmental factor. Accordingly, the environment can influence the organization culturally—employing accepted values as a mechanism to form beliefs and myths (Deal and Kennedy, 1982).

Strong evidence exists suggesting that public perceptions of adult education are changing. Although the precise quality and quantity of these changes are difficult to pinpoint, this information can be understood in relation to certain indicators which are manifestations of change.

Factors Influencing Public Perceptions

The public image of adult education is an amalgamation of various individual and group understandings of the field, shared values and beliefs, the perceived relationship between public needs and adult education's potential for appropriate responses, and the nature of conditions and situations within which people find themselves. When these conditions are transformed, public perceptions can be expected to have a catalytic effect upon alterations in adult education practice. Among the key areas of practice, in this regard, are adult education resource base development (Dahl, 1980), particapation levels (Bock, 1980), and program development.

The forces influencing public perception of adult education have been categorized in several ways. According to Wright (1980), there are three basic types of relevant forces: changes in social systems, changes in cultural systems, and changes in personal systems. These categories represent a hierarchy wherein each stratum influences each of the other stratums. As an example of the interplay among such forces and their effects, consider the advancements of technology in relation to dwindling resources in the world. Or ponder the effects of racial, ethnic, political, and religious upheavals on a society in which individuals are likely to become more alienated as their opportunities to participate meaningfully in government decline (Boone, 1980).

These are not the only factors influencing public perceptions of adult education. There are other profound changes currently in progress. Population shifts and family changes are two that stand out. In recent years, migration patterns have been mixed. Although many are still fleeing certain urban areas, there are other parts of the country where a renewed interest in city dwelling can be observed. Mobility among the unemployed, for example, appears to be declining because of factors such as two-income families. Divorce has become a serious concern because of its unpredictable effects upon family members. Although these examples serve notice of ongoing change, the specific products of these alterations remain uncertain.

The condition which probably most directly relates to changes in public perceptions of adult education is the accelerating rate at which knowledge is being created and discovered. Today, more than at any other period in history, there is an almost bewildering amount of scientific discovery and technological development taking place. Frandson (1980), in commenting that the time between completion of formal education and obsolescence is getting progressively shorter, indicates that the college degree is rapidly being considered the beginning of the education of a professional, rather than the culminating event.

Another key factor in the public perception of adult education is the nature of adults' attitudes toward their continuing ability to learn throughout life (Lowe, 1982). The nature of this attitude, in turn, affects such significant elements as the availability of adult education resources (Dahl, 1980) and actual participation levels (Bock, 1980).

Adult education in the eyes of the public also is influenced by the relationship between continued educational development and employment prospects. The impact of this influence is different for various demographic groupings. Women, for example, increasingly view adult education participation as a means toward a career (Feeney, 1980). Older adults do not see themselves as students and do not embrace either the vocational emphasis of adult education or the status involved in earning a diploma (Marcus and Havinghurst, 1980).

The effects of history constitute additional forces influencing public perceptions. Both the rate and nature of change in the practice of adult education, coupled with the public's view of this change, are related considerations. As examples of this phenomenon, consider the following obstacles to an accurate public image:

- No common image is accepted for adult education.
- Adult education is considered a luxury rather than a necessity.
- Many continue to cling to the notion that education is solely for children.
- Many continue to believe that the primary function of adult education is to provide vocational training (Cotton, 1960).

Even though these barriers were reported about twenty-five years ago, they have not been totally eradicated.

Given the existence of such dynamic and interrelated factors, the question becomes one of effect. How does the public view adult education? To what extent have the aforementioned factors influenced the public's perceptions of adult education? What evidence exists to substantiate these influences?

Public Perceptions of Adult Education

Adult education is viewed as a legitimate and recognized field of social practice. It has developed naturally and orderly (Luke, 1969). There have been few cataclysmic events in the evolution of adult education which have altered radically its nature, function, or promise. Within this reasonably predictable pattern of development, however, there have been changes in public understanding, awareness, and expectation. These changes can best be understood by examining four categories of variables related to the nature of the public perception of adult education: awareness, interest, and participation; conceptual understanding; programmatic integration; and financing.

Awareness, Interest, and Participation. It is estimated that at least half of all American adults are engaged in education (Eyre, 1983). This unprecedented level of participation in organized adult education is no doubt the result of the complex interplay among changing public perceptions and societal, cultural, and personal dynamics. Prominent among these dynamics is the increased acceptance of two major concepts—lifelong education and the learning society.

The idea of the learning society is likely to continue to gain momentum and to influence future adult education participation patterns. As portrayed in the report prepared by the National Commission on Excellence in Education, entitled *A Nation at Risk* (1983), the learning society is not unlike a societal ethic which places renewed emphasis on granting each citizen the opportunity to develop his mind to full capacity from early childhood through adulthood.

Some adult authorities contend that adult educational involvement and participation are actually much more prolific than current estimates. Tough (1979), for example, indicates that almost everyone participates in adult education. He views adult education as encompassing the adult learning project or "a major, highly deliberate effort to gain certain knowledge and skill." Tough estimates that it is not uncommon for individuals to invest seven hundred hours in as few as one or two or as many as twenty learning projects per year. Although less than 1 percent of these learning efforts are undertaken for formal credit, it is clear that many of them would fall in the category of organized learning activities.

Adult education awareness and participation also are influenced to a great degree by practical and deliberate means designed specifically to affect public perceptions. Bock (1980) indicates that increasing public awareness and respect for adult education are being cultivated by providing relevant, affordable programs at convenient locations and times. She also contends that such measures serve to combat unfamiliarity with available adult education opportunities, one of the major barriers to active participation.

A final consideration related to adult education interest, awareness, and participation is the subtle change in strategy for interfacing with the public. In the past, considerable effort was extended toward promotion and publicity (Rauch, 1969) and public image and understanding (Cotton, 1960). The major emphasis of these approaches was to improve public information by making basic data available. Today, the distribution of accurate information remains important; however, this distribution now occurs more frequently as part of a comprehensive marketing approach. Contemporary marketing strategies are more aggressive, more inclusive (more than presenting facts), and based upon concepts and practices pioneered and used in private industry. These more sophisticated marketing approaches have contributed to the changes in public perceptions of adult education.

Conceptual Understanding. The fact that both formal and informal education pervades virtually all aspects of adult life is serving to refine public perceptions. As an integral dimension of major societal and community institutions, adult education is continually being appraised, scrutinized, and clarified. Although personal experiences remain the primary source of assessment, the sheer volume of adult education in America is now playing a key role in shaping public perceptions.

There is additional evidence that public perceptions of adult education are being altered. The following indicators identified by Eyre (1983) support this contention:

> Each state and territory of the United States has an administrative staff responsible for adult education.
>
> Graduate work in adult education, extension, and continuing education thrusts are available in many American institutions of higher education.
>
> Public willingness to support adult education through taxes and consumer willingness to support it through tuition payments and fees are increasing.
>
> Adult education as an undertaking of noneducational institutions is rapidly expanding.
>
> The emphasis of adult education programs is moving away from academic subjects toward life problems and societal concerns.

Off-campus community services provided by colleges and public schools are given greater emphasis.

On the basis of these indicators, one can conclude that the public perceptions of adult education are becoming increasingly favorable and more broadly oriented.

Programmatic Integration. Both the quantity and quality of adult education efforts continue to increase. Not only are more and more institutions becoming involved, but these organizations are also devoting more time and money to planning, conducting, and evaluating adult education activities. Amidst this whirlwind of activity are two subtle, but discernible, changes in organizational attitudes.

First, organizations are integrating adult education into formal organizational operations. The concept of an organization within an organization was discussed earlier in the book. This trend is evolving in private as well as in public sectors and seems to be accelerating. This vertical integration of adult education is based upon the belief that continued development of personnel is directly related to individual productivity and, therefore, organizational effectiveness. Such intraorganizational adult education, according to Nadler (1980), consists of three basic types of experience:

Experience	*Emphasis*
Training	Present job learning
Education	Different job learning
Development	Future directions learning

Second, there are greater efforts to synchronize and integrate adult education activities across organizational lines. The intent of this form of integration is to provide maximum benefit and opportunity for education consumers. Shaw (1969) noted that adult educators were moving away from considering adult education as separate from elementary, secondary, and higher education. The goal has become one way of integrating adult education with other formal programs in order to generate flexibility in continuing education. The programmatic integration of adult education, vertically and horizontally, may prove to be the single most significant development in contemporary adult education. This trend, as the product of changing public perceptions of adult education, will continue to abet the legitimacy of adult education and to enhance its public image.

Financing. As adult education continues to become understood and accepted by the public and integrated into the fabric of institutions, organizations, and agencies, it is evident that the funding allocated for such purposes also is increasing. Although it is difficult to pinpoint and monitor the extent of adult education financing, it is clear that adult education is big business.

Eyre (1983) reports that over $2.1 billion is paid annually by individual adult education course participants, and billions of additional dollars are generated by other organizations. Boyer (1983) indicates that funds involved in education within the private corporate sector are considerably greater. Corporate education is becoming a booming business.

> Costing over $30 billion annually, there are now about 130 corporations offering 2,000 such courses.

Also of note is the increasing interest the federal government is paying to adult education. In particular, fiscal considerations for supporting growth are becoming more frequent in Congress. Although much of this interest is restricted to basic adult education programs, there appears to be increasing acknowledgement that other types of programs also merit fiscal support. Knox (1986) points out that as adult education becomes more prevalent, the issues of financing will become more pressing. In particular, planners must concern themselves with two fiscally related issues: (1) how to serve those adults who are hard to reach with organized programming, and (2) how subsidies can be broadened to cover nonoccupational programs aimed at improving the quality of life.

THE CONCEPT OF LIFELONG EDUCATION FOR EVERYONE

Acceptance of education as a lifelong process has grown in recent years. Even though this view is accepted conceptually, especially by professional educators, the transition of this belief to actual practice may take years to accomplish. The relationship between lifelong education and society is complex. First, the natural evolution of lifelong education contributes to the rapidity and complexity of societal change. Second, the concept provides a pragmatic intervention for mediating such change. To completely understand the relationship of lifelong education and adult education, one must consider lifelong education in three basic ways: in isolation, within the context of societal dynamics, and as an increasingly important life-style. Although some argue that lifelong education is a reality regardless of public perceptions (for example, Brookfield, 1986), philosophical acceptance remains a critical factor. The cultural proclivity to view education as a youth activity remains vigorous in many parts of the world.

The Nature of Lifelong Education

Lifelong education is not a uniquely American concept. The idea has received attention in educational literature during past decades. The extent to which a precise international semantic interpretation of lifelong education exists is obscured by various national terms associated with the concept. For example, lifelong education is simultaneously referred to in different countries as "recurrent education," "extra-mural education," "permanent education," "further education," "adult education," "continuing education," and "extension education" (Williams, 1977). On a general level, however, these terms can be regarded as synonymous with lifelong education.

The concept of lifelong education has the individual as its primary focus. Any definition of the term should consider its direct relationship to the continuous growth and development of people. Although the primacy of the individual is evident, the concept also has direct implications for educational and other organizations. The most significant definitions of lifelong education are those which address the individual and institutional dimensions of this concept simultaneously. For example, these definitions cite the purposes and effects for the individual and for the organization (or society, or community).

This concept also can be examined by an analysis of its two basic components. According to Parkyn (1973), the lifelong aspect of the concept is based on the view that modern conditions and discovery of knowledge are changing so rapidly that education during childhood and adolescence alone cannot possibly suffice for a lifetime. Information and knowledge are coming into existence at a rate that requires continuous learning. The education aspect of the concept involves instruction as an essential element to achieve this continuous learning.

The basic rationale for lifelong education is related to the inevitability of change. Social alterations and technological advancements render conventional education more restrictive than at any other time in history. Moreover, it seems clear that the information and knowledge explosion will continue to accelerate. Given this scenario, lifelong education becomes the vehicle for producing educable (as opposed to educated) and adaptable people who are able to select and control their own pattern of educational development (Parkyn, 1973). A critical consideration in this regard is the development and maintenance of an interest in learning:

> One of the greatest products of a meaningful education is the intellectual curiosity that leads men and women to continued learning and makes them eager to learn as the experience of life reveals areas of ignorance, (Hesburgh, Miller, and Wharton, 1973, p. 26)

The concept of lifelong education represents a departure from the standard one-dimensional roles of teachers and students. The students encompass the entire population and not just youth. In addition, everyone is a potential teacher. Given this educational agenda, planning and programming must be flexible in terms of time, space, usage patterns, age, and admission constraints (Lowe, 1982). From the organizational perspective, lifelong learning requires an inordinate amount of coordination. This coordination not only involves more effective articulation among the various parts of an organization, but it often requires linkages among a number of organizations (Parkyn, 1973). This coordination and cooperation spawn new delivery systems. Therefore, the future configurations of lifelong education may take many different forms—all the more reason that the administrator of adult education ought to acquire the ability to function in a variety of environments.

Lifelong Education Forces

Acceptance of lifelong education is being influenced by a host of societal trends, developments, and conditions. Many of these forces are interrelated, and even though they have their beginnings in earlier periods, the pace at which they are developing must be considered revolutionary. Among the most significant are radical demographic changes; technological developments; social trends; and new relationships among work, leisure, and education.

According to Chimene (1983), the adult population in the United States will increase by 9 percent between 1984 and 1996. A longer lifespan is primarily responsible for this forecast. As life expands, so does the percentage of one's life which falls into the adult stage. Approximately 75 percent of life is lived as an adult (Kidd, 1973). This cumulation of adults is likely to increase participation in adult education by over 30 percent by the mid-1990s (Chimene, 1983).

Technological advancements also abet the proliferation of lifelong education. This is occurring in two notable ways. First, as the manifestations of science become an integral aspect of adult life, the need to understand and effectively use technology becomes critical. Scientific developments will occur at an accelerated pace, and this fact also illuminates the necessity of continuous learning. Second, this same technology is making aspects of lifelong learning possible. For example, the combination of television and computer technology resulting in interactive video makes individualized learning in the home an option in today's world (Deshler and Gay, 1983).

Social trends constitute an additional force molding lifelong education. Changing learner needs, tastes, and participation patterns serve as examples. Many older learners, for instance, show greater interest in organized learning experiences if they have an option to participate on a part-time basis (Ferris,

1974). Thus, as institutions become more flexible in responding to societal changes, the process of lifelong education is cultivated. As far back as 1974, it was estimated that over half of the post secondary students in America were part-time students (Boyer, 1974). This figure continues to grow as many adults past the age of twenty-five attempt to continue their education. Even noneducational organizations have responded to social trends, creating opportunities for learning for employees and the general population. Here too, participation and programs have increased (Knox, 1977). Closely related to social forces are cultural influences; values and beliefs are altered to provide a more favorable environment in which lifelong learning can be actualized. The cultural element is more complex than the social, and it is viewed by some as the amalgamation of all forces.

A final force worth mentioning is the relationship among work, leisure, and education. In the past, these components were segregated chronologically (O'Toole, 1974). Education was synonymous with childhood and youth, work was a central function of adulthood, and retirement (a period of primarily leisure) was associated with old age. Today, these segments of life are less autonomous. Increases in the volume of leisure, the incidence of career and vocational change, and the subsequent need for education have disrupted the historical and static pattern of life's dimensions. The trend toward integration of individual vocational, leisure, and educational develement requires access to learning opportunities throughout life. The importance of these issues is apparent in recent research efforts in adult education which are attempting to link work-related problems to educational opportunities (for example, Dean, 1986; Clark, 1986).

The forces influencing lifelong education have been isolated here for purposes of discussion. In reality, however, these forces are inextricably related and mutually reinforcing. Their serious consideration within the context of education has given momentum to a new value orientation and, perhaps, cultural imperative—the learning society. Naisbitt (1982) notes that Americans are moving from the short-term considerations of completing their training at the end of high school or college to lifelong education and retraining. He predicts that the concept of education will be reconceptualized during the next decade.

The Learning Society

The idea of the learning society also has aroused curiosity in recent years. Proponents of lifelong education appear to see the learning society as both a natural outgrowth of the increasing acceptance of education throughout life and, at the same time, its prerequisite cultural ethic. At the core of the learning society is a new level of understanding, appreciation, and respect for education and its critical importance in the continuing development of the social order. A practical implication of the attitudinal metamorphosis required for the learning society is that active participation in all types of educational activity will increase significantly.

The learning society described by Lowe (1982) is one in which education is a principal and pervasive human activity. Specifically, the existence of the learning society will be characterized by the presence of the following conditions:

- The continuous expansion, appraisal, and universal dissemination of knowledge
- Continuous learning throughout childhood, youth, and adulthood
- The widespread involvement of social institutions at all levels in educational endeavors
- The accelerated participation of economic organizations in all types of education.

This interpretation is consistent with that of Hesburgh, Miller, and Wharton (1973). Both interpretations suggest that myriad educational opportunities are available inside and outside formal educational institutions.

Although the term *learning society* could lead to a conclusion that societal needs constitute the most basic concern, such a judgment would be in error. Several prominent educational theorists (for example, Hesburgh, Miller, and Wharton, 1973; Williams, 1977) indicate that the needs of learners are, in fact, most important. Others (for example, Boshier and Nickerson, 1983) contend that adult education is more society oriented. This lack of consensus regarding the focus of the learning society sustains ambiguity (Kidd, 1973). Today, a good many practitioners accept the notion that education ought to address the needs of individuals, organizations, and society in unison.

From a pragmatic perspective, the learning society is a utopian concept. There is evidence, nevertheless, that society is evolving in the direction of this goal. It is predicted, for example, that by the turn of the century there will be a significant increase in adults engaging in some form of education. The educational resources of museums, religious institutions, and other organizations are playing a more essential role today in providing services. Collectively these opportunities make adult education much more accessible than in the past.

For some organizations, especially private corporations, adult education has not been circumscribed by traditions: that is, programming for adults is not limited by concerns and practices associated with eucating younger person

Educational institutions, on the other hand, are encountering more complex effects of the progression to a learning society. The effects upon the four-year colleges and universities serve as an excellent example. In some institutions of higher education, change to meet the needs for a learning society has been virtually imperceptible. In a second group of institutions, lifelong education has served as a guiding principle for renewal and has followed an evolutionary process (Williams, 1977). Finally, there is a third group consisting of institutions in which change has been significant and abrupt. Parkyn (1973) suggests that deficiencies in many colleges and universities have been so great that only radical and complete reform, as exhibited in this third group, could meet the needs that would come with the actualization of the learning society. Today, many continue to agree with his position. This is true in large measure because the extent of institutional change generated by lifelong education remains uneven. This fact becomes very clear when one examines the vast differences in philosophies and operating procedures among the several thousand institutions of higher education in America. Some have become extremely flexible and actively pursue the adult student. Others resist change and function much as they did fifty years ago—catering only to the seventeen- to twenty-two-year-old student.

THE NEED FOR RESEARCH

Historically, adult educators have been oriented more toward the pragmatic aspects of program development. The theoretical facets have received far less attention (Krietlow, 1970). This condition is largely the product of necessity, that is, programs had to be formulated rapidly. Scholars and practitioners devoted much of their efforts to meeting needs in the marketplace. Earlier in this book, the relationship of research to theory and organizational development was discussed in detail. As previously indicated, adult education is both a social practice and an area of academic study. In this latter category, the extension of research and the application of research have become essential to the future growth of the field.

The Importance of Adult Education Research

The literature in adult education contains many recommendations for increasing scientific inquiry (for example, Overstreet, 1936; Lindeman, 1961; Hiemstra, 1976). Krietlow (1970) points out that research and theory development are prime foundational characteristics of accepted disciplines, and these two functions have been overt challenges to adult educators since the 1920s.

Despite this recognition of need, research and theory building have not been fully used either as a source of academic study or as a basis for improved practice. Perhaps the widest gap between theory and practice exists in the area of program planning (Brookfield, 1986).

The lack of critical research studies designed to analyze the prerequisites for the continued development of adult education in general has been one of the most glaring weaknesses of the profession (Rubenson, 1982). Lowe (1982), for example, points out that there is an urgent need for the field of adult education to adopt a realistic research and development policy. The neglect of research, according to Lowe, has resulted in ignored antecedents, repeated mistakes, and wasted efforts.

The importance of research is underscored by the rapidity of change which characterizes this century. Despite this realization, much of adult education continues to emulate and resemble conventional education for youth. Fortunately, practitioners are discovering that many of the assumptions of conventional education are invalidated in adult education by technological and societal changes. They are discovering this because they are mired in many conventional practices (Parkyn, 1973).

The future portends even more complex organizations and programs. For this reason, research and theory building increase in value. The gravity of research is exemplified in a study conducted by Merriam and Mullins (1981). In studying traditional approaches to programming, the researchers examined the effects of using certain principles upon various subgroups. They discovered notable differences among groups of adult students, suggesting that single-minded approaches to program planning presented limitations for some of the students. In this instance, the use of Havinghurst's developmental tasks was the organizing principle being studied. In essence, different approaches may produce varying levels of success. Brookfield (1986) fortifies such findings with his excellent criticism of the use of technical approaches to program planning in adult education. Without such newly acquired information, the profession would be mired in generalizations and dependent upon simplistic models of program planning. Research and craft knowledge provide the only two vehicles for overcoming stagnation.

Research Directions

Adult education research has been hampered by the diversity of graduate study and practice (Weaver and Kowalski, 1987). The lack of standard program sponsorship, program design, purpose, methodology, and intended outcomes affects the generalizability and significance of research. But such diversity is not likely to dissipate. Despite wishful thinking by some, it is unlikely that adult education can be reduced to uniform practices (Newman, 1979). Yet it is myopic to accept arguments presented by those who believe that there is no common core of knowledge in adult education (for example, James, 1981). Such a conclusion is actually self-incriminating. If no common core of knowledge exists, why then do universities offer degrees in the field?

A review of research in adult education indicates that, although quantity and quality remain problematic, a few interrelated areas should constitute major foci. These areas include the adult as a learner (Long, 1983), adult education programming (Grabowski, 1980), and the adult education enterprise (Long, 1983). In addition, the practice of adult education touches upon a host of related disciplines (such as anthropology, sociology, and psychology). Research which integrates related disciplines into adult education has been advocated by a number of scholars (for example, Grabowski, 1980; Rubenson, 1982). Knox (1980), however, perceives a danger in the unrestricted application of behavioral science research:

> Most formal research relevant to adult education comes from other disciplines such as psychology or sociology, but often such research does not apply directly to practice or provide a blueprint for decision making by practitioners. (p. 3).

Over twenty-five years ago, Krietlow (1960) identified six categories of research which are essentially unique to adult education:

1. Individual and group needs and wants
2. Adult education agency plans and purposes
3. Adult education and community resources
4. Adult education agency operations
5. Instructional methods for adults
6. Adult education outcomes

Since these suggestions were made, there has been some notable progress in addressing them. In 1980, Knox developed a list of eight areas he believed were relevant to adult education research:

1. Program objectives and activities
2. Methodology and materials
3. Program evaluation
4. Adult education participation

5. Resource usage

6. Adult education personnel

7. Adult education leadership

8. Organizational considerations

The final one, organizational considerations, is the nucleus of this book. Two newer areas which have attracted the attention of researchers are studies of comparative adult education (Kidd, 1981) and studies of brain functioning among adult learners (for example, Even and Lux, 1983). Comparative studies examine the practice of adult education in different countries (and thus different societal settings). Future directions in adult education research may include cross-cultural studies, strategies for self-directed learning, and studies of models appropriate for training adult educators to work in educational and other organizational settings (Boshier, 1981).

Funding Adult Education Research

The future of research activities in adult education hinges upon a multitude of factors. Determining who will be responsible for financing such efforts is foremost. Given the complexity of program offerings and the diversity in sponsorship, many practitioners are looking to the federal government for fiscal support. This appears to be a rational vision, particularly if this country is to make a long-term investment in the concept of adult education (Moore, 1981).

It is most unlikely that all future research needs can be supported by federal grants. States and individual organizations ought to be willing to assume a portion of the burden. Given the interest accorded by private industry in adult education, grants and funded projects from this sector of the economy may prove to be quite fertile. In large measure, increased fiscal support is dependent upon a link between adult education and the economic and social factors which are beneficial to the growth of American society.

MAINSTREAMING ADULT EDUCATION

The term *mainstreaming* is most frequently used in the area of special education. It denotes a process of placing children with special needs into regular programs whenever isolated placement cannot be professionally justified. For example, a mildly retarded child may be mainstreamed into a regular physical education class. The purpose is to expose the child to the "real" world as often as possible and to educate him or her in the least restrictive environment (Malone and Flowers, 1980).

Here, mainstreaming refers to the deliberate infusion of adult education into the mission, philosophy, and operations of various organizations. This concept entails more than the mere adoption of program(s). It involves the following:

- The cultivation of organizational values which exemplify respect for individual adults, individuality, and democracy

- The recognition of the importance of continuing education throughout life

- The establishment of an educational ethic as the overriding purpose of education

- The establishment of an organizational system of operation within which adult education is considered equally as important as the education of children and youth

There is little question that adult education is yet to become fully legitimized within many educational institutions, let alone in organizations maintaining a primary purpose other than education. Thus, adult education frequently remains outside the mainstream of eductional discussions and considerations in America (Charters, 1981).

This isolation is not common in all countries. In Germany, for example, adult education is accorded a status closely approximating conventional education. The integration of adult education into a more encompassing mission appears to be partially dependent upon culture. In some countries, it may be difficult to adopt foreign institutional patterns and organizational arrangements for schooling. Accordingly, adult education integration may be more suitable and likely in certain cultures (Adieseshia, 1975).

The issue of mainstreaming adult education is also directly related to the concept of lifelong education. If lifelong learning actually gains philosophical acceptance, the integration of adult education into a variety of organizations is apt to occur through a natural evolutionary process (Charters, 1981). Given this potentiality, adult education could be transformed from a segregated activity designed to compensate for deficiencies in the "normal" educational process to the crowning stage of a continuous and integrated system. Mainstreaming is therefore most relevant to the growth of adult education and the sophistication of program planning.

SUMMARY

The forces affecting adult education are many and varied. They do not conform to a predictable pattern, nor are they entirely controllable. Foremost among such forces are changing public perceptions of adult education, lifelong education, the concept of the learning society, adult education research needs, and the future mainstreaming of adult education into organizations.

Most adult educators recognize the evolutionary nature of their field of practice. Linking new knowledge, improvements, and alterations to the art and science of program development should produce benefits for the practitioner. This chapter has emphasized those processes that are likely to affect the planning and organization of programs.

As the American public accepts the need to cope with societal and technological changes, education will become a necessary process for all citizens. This realization should result in the mobilization of many institutions to address the demands for more organized educational programs for adult students. It also should spawn resources that permit research and theory building to become primary catalysts for the continued growth of adult education as a social practice and a professional field of study.

FOR FURTHER DISCUSSION

1. Differentiate between societal change and cultural change. How do these changes affect adult education in the United States?

2. Discuss the major attributes of a "learning society."

3. What are some reasons that taxpayers may be reluctant to support adult education?

4. What are the advantages of integrating adult education into the culture of an organization?

5. Identify the similarities and differences in the following three terms:

   - Adult education
   - Lifelong education
   - Community education

   How has each been affected by American society in the last twenty years

6. Has diversity of practice hindered research in adult education? W⸍ why not?

7.   What changes will be necessary to mainstream adult education into American life?

REFERENCES

Adieseshia, M. (1975). Introduction. In C. Bennett, J. Kidd, and J. Kulich (Eds.), *Comparative studies in adult education: An anthology* (pp. 1–14). Syracuse, NY: Syracuse University Press.

Bock, L. (1980). Participation. In A. Knox and Associates (Eds.), *Developing, administering and evaluating adult education* (pp. 124–153). San Francisco: Jossey-Bass.

Boone, E. (1980). Introduction: Serving needs through adult education. In E. Boone, R. Shearon, E. White, and Associates (Eds.), *Serving personal and community needs through adult education* (pp. 1–9. San Francisco: Jossey-Bass.

Boshier, R. (1981). Adult education: Issues of the future. In B. Krietlow and Associates (Eds.), *Examining controversies in adult education* (pp. 235–255). San Francisco: Jossey-Bass.

Boshier, R., and Nickerson, V. (1983). Purposes of adult education: An instrument and model. In R. Cervero, M. Collins, M. Even, and N. Robbins (Eds.), *Proceedings: Twenty fourth annual adult education research conference* (pp. 26–31). Montreal, Quebec: Concordia University, Adult Education Program and Centre for Continuing Education.

Boyer, E. (1974). Breaking the youth ghetto. In D. Vermilye (Ed.), *Lifelong learners— a new clientele for higher education* (pp. 4–11). San Francisco: Jossey-Bass.

———. (1983), May 25). Opinion. *Chronicle of Higher Education,* p. 32.

Brookfield, S. (1986). *Understanding and facilitating adult learning.* San Francisco: Josey-Bass.

Charters, A. (1981). Learning from each other. In A. Charters and Associates (Eds.), *Comparing adult education worldwide* (pp.–17). San Francisco: Jossey-Bass.

Chimene, D. (1983). Beyond 1984: Projecting participation in adult education. In R. Cervero, M. Collins, M. Even, and N. Robbins (Eds.), *Proceedings: Twenty fourth annual adult education research conferencee* (pp.51–56). Montreal, Quebec: Concordia University, Adult Education Program and Centre for Continuing Education.

Clark, R. (1986). Burnout and associated factors among administrator/mid-managers of the cooperative extension service of the north central region. *Proceedings, 1986 Midwest research-to-practice conference in adult, community, and continuing education* (pp. 19–24). Muncie, IN: Ball State University.

ton, T. (1960). Public understanding of adult education. In M. Knowles (Ed.), *Handbook of adult education in the United States* (pp. 129–137). Chicago: Adult Education Association of the USA.

Dahl, D. (1980). Resources. In A. Knowles and Associates (Eds.), *Developing, administering and evaluating adult education (pp. 154–180)*. San Francisco: Jossey-Bass.

Deal, T., and Kennedy, A. (1982). *Corporate cultures*. Reading, MA: Addison-Wesley.

Dean, G. (1986). Factors affecting displaced workers' participation in education and training programs. *Proceedings, 1986 Midwest research-to-practice conference in adult, community, and continuing education* (pp. 31–36). Muncie, IN: Ball State University.

Deshler, D., and Gay, G. (1983). Educational potential of interactive video technology: An evaluation of a pilot project. In R. Cervero, M. Collins, M. Even, and N. Robbins (Eds.), *Proceedings: Twenty fourth annual adult education research conference* (pp. 81–86). Montreal, Quebec: Concordia University, Adult Education Program and Centre for Continuing Education.

Even, M., and Lux, T. (1983). New test for brain hemisphere preference: Implications for in-class procedures and instructional techniques. In R. Cervero, M. Collins, M. Even, and N. Robbins (Eds.), *Proceedings: Twenty fourth annual adult education research conference* (pp. 93–98). Montreal, Quebec: Concordia University, Adult Education Program and Centre for Continuing Education.

Eyre, G. (1983, September). From the executive director. *AACE Newsletter*, p. 4.

Feeney, H. (1980). Women's education. In E. Boone, R. Shearon, E. White, and Associates (Eds.), *Serving personal and community needs through adult education* (pp. 47–60. San Francisco: Jossey-Bass.

Ferris, W. (1974). The quiet revolution. In D. Vermilye (Ed.), *Lifelong learners—A new clientele for higher education (pp. 1–3)*. San Francisco: Jossey-Bass.

Frandson, P. (1980). Continuing education in the professions. In E. Boone, R. Shearon, E. White, and Associates (Eds.), *Serving personal and community needs through adult education* (pp. 61–81). San Francisco: Jossey-Bass.

Grabowski, S. (1980). Trends in graduate research. In H. Long and R. Hiemstra (Eds.), *Changing approaches to studying adult education* (pp. 119–128). San Francisco: Jossey-Bass.

Hesburgh, T., Miller, P., and Wharton, C. (1973). *Patterns for lifelong learning*. San Francisco: Jossey-Bass.

Hiemstra, R. (1976). *Lifelong learning*. Lincoln, NE: Professional Educators Publications.

James, W. (1981). Certification's unfeasible and undesirable. In B. W. Kreitlow and Associates (Eds.), *Examining controversies in adult education* (pp. 84–95). Francisco: Jossey-Bass.

Kidd, J. (1973). *How adults learn*. Chicago: Follett.

———. (1981). Research. In W. Charters and Associates Eds.), *Comparing tion worldwide* (pp. 218–239). San Francisco: Jossey-Bass.

Knox, A. (1977). *Adult development and learning*. San Francisco:

_____. (1980). Future directions. In A. Knox (Ed.), *Developing, administering and evaluating adult education (pp. 247–262)*. San Francisco: Jossey-Bass.

_____. (1986) Who should finance adult education? *Eastern Education Journal, 18*(2), 8–13.

Krietlow, B. (1960). Research in adult education. In M. Knowles (Ed.), *Handbook of adult education in the United States* (pp. 106–116). Chicago: Adult Education Association of the USA.

_____. (1970). Research and theory. In R. Smith, G. Aker, and J. Kidd (Eds.), *Handbook of adult education* (pp. 106–116.) New York: Macmillan.

Lindeman, E. (1961). *The meaning of adult education*. Montreal: Harvest House.

Long, H. (1983). Characteristics of adult education research reported at the adult education research conference, 1971–1980, *Adult Education, 33*(2), 79–96.

Lowe, J. (1982). *The education of adults: A world perspective*. Paris: United Nations Educational, Scientific and Cultural Organizations.

Luke, R. (1969). The development of public support for adult education. In N. Shaw (Ed.), *Administration of continuing education* (pp. 12–26). Washington, DC: National Association of Public School Adult Education.

Malone, V., and Flowers, W. (1980). Education for economic and social development. In E. Boone, R. Shearon, E. White, and Associates (Eds.), *Serving personal and community needs through adult education* (pp. 129–146). San Francisco: Jossey-Bass.

Marcus, E., and Havinghurst, R. (1980). Education for the aging. In E. Boone, R. Shearon, E. White, and Associates (Eds.), *Serving personal and community needs through adult education* (pp. 22–40). San Francisco: Jossey-Bass.

Merriam, S., and Mullins, L. (1981). Havinghurst's adult developmental tasks: A study of their importance relative to income, age and sex. *Adult Education, 13,* 123–141.

Moore, A. (1981). The federal government must assume a leadership role. In B. Krietlow and Associates (Eds.), *Examining controversies in adult education* (pp. 208–214). San Francisco: Jossey-Bass.

Nadler, L. (1980). Human resource development for managers. In E. Boone, R. Shearon, E. White, and Associates (Eds.), *Serving personal and community needs through adult education* (pp. 82–96). San Francisco: Jossey-Bass.

_____itt, J. (1982). *Megatrends*. New York: Warner Books.

_____ional Commission on Excellence in Education (198_). *A nation at risk*. _____shington, D. C.: U. S. Government Printing Office.

_____ (1979). *The poor cousin: A study of adult education*. _____ton: Allen and

O''foole, J. (1974). Education, work and quality of life. In D. Vermilye (Ed.), *Lifelong learners—A new clientele for higher education* (pp. 12–21). San Francisco: Jossey-Bass.

Overstreet, H. (1936). No previous training required. *Journal of Adult Education 8*, 241–246.

Parkyn, G. (1973). *Towards a conceptual model of life-long education*. Paris: United Nations Educational, Scientific and Cultural Organization.

Rauch, D. (1969). Community relations, promotion and publicity. In N. Shaw (Ed.), *Administration of continuing education* (pp. 200–215). Washington, DC: National Association for Public School Adult Education.

Rubenson, K. (1982). Adult education research: In quest of a map of the territory. *Adult Education, 32*(2), 57–74.

Shaw, N. (1969). A look ahead—patterns and trends. In N, Shaw (Ed.), *Administration of continuing education* (pp. 392–393). Washington, DC: National Association for Public School Adult Education.

Tough, A. (1979). *The adult's learning projects: A fresh approach to theory and practice in adult education*. Toronto: Ontario Institute for Studies in Education.

Weaver, R., and Kowalski, T. (1987). The case for program accreditation of doctoral degrees in adult education. *Lifelong Learning, 10*(7), 14–15, 26–27.

Williams, G. (1977). *Towards lifelong education: A new role for higher education institutions*. Paris: United Nations Educational, Scientific and Cultural Organization.

Wright, J. (1980). Community learning: A frontier for adult education. In R. Boyd, J. Apps, and Associates (Eds.), *Redefining the discipline of adult education* (pp. 99–125). San Francisco: Jossey-Bass.

CHAPTER 14

Future Challenges

Futurism has become a common word for many Americans. Ever since the mid 1970s, there has been an obsession with attempting to predict tomorrow. In large measure, this interest is generated by the rapid changes occurring in the social, economic, and occupational lives of most citizens. These alterations threaten many persons; not surprisingly, they generate an intense interest in trying to forecast where society is going.

The love affair with futurism is clearly evident in the number of commercial television productions designed to entice consumers to invest in various information sources which supposedly have predictive powers. Ranging from stock market projections to anticipating which card will be next from a casino blackjack deck, packaged forecasting has become big business. Regardless of whether one considers futurism an art, a science, or crystal ball gazing, it has emerged as a component in many fields of study. Economics, sociology, and psychology are three of the more active disciplines.

The commercialization of futurism ought not obviate its value to academic studies. Skeptics believe that prediction is little more than a manifestation of the adage, "saying it makes it so." Academics are only beginning to sense the benefits of emergent, creative thinking with regard to program planning. The value of infusing futurism into the study of adult education leadership lies not so much in preparing practitioners and organizations to adjust to tomorrow but rather in its enlightening attributes related to how the future is yet to created. This perspective is crucial to eradicating the greatest barrier to imp planning in adult education. As Simpson (1982) points out, and as Bro (1986) discusses, the continued dependence upon simplistic technic deters planners from fining adult education. The previous chap the importance of this refinement, and administrators who are or grams are critical the process. Program planners can follow t

199

can perceive themselves as evaluators of conditions and prepare their programs to adjust to those conditions. This approach constitutes a form of environmental determinism. Conversely, they can merge planning with philosophical direction. Futurism then becomes a critical element for directing programs toward a prescribed concept of adult education in American life.

As a field of social service, adult education is still in its early stages of development. There is common agreement that adult education has evolved into an amalgam that includes diverse subject matter areas and numerous program divisions (Hoare, 1982). But the foundational aspects of adult education, those that entail values related to the social, psychological, and emotional aspects of education, remain somewhat imprecise. Establishing a national agenda, for example, has become a high priority for many scholars in adult education. Such an agenda could provide philosophical parameters that are relevant to all ventures in this field of human service.

One requisite to confronting the future is the identification of those forces which will bear most heavily upon moving practice to a level at which individual and societal needs equal organizational needs. Within the practice of adult education, some of these factors have been analyzed extensively, and others are only beginning to become apparent. This chapter addresses five dynamic issues that could make planning more scholarly and congruent with the values of a democratic society. Literature in adult education contains abundant information about the growing popularity of the field and the more obvious reasons that America is embracing lifelong education. Frequently, this information is merely descriptive and used to verify that adult education is a growing enterprise. But, what will be the implications of these developments with regard to the shape and direction of organized learning activities in the next decade? Will these factors make program planning fertile ground for refinement, or will they ensure the perpetuation of past practice?

CHANGING NEEDS

One factor that is vital to the future of program planning is the estimated demand for adult education. It is universally accepted that the demand will increase, but there are differences of opinion regarding the form this demand will take. For instance, there are those who believe that a greater percentage of education will occur on an individual basis. This forecast is predicated on the rapid deployment of technology, especially the home computer. Others see that social factors will continue to drive the demand for organized learning experiences upward. Still others believe that the greatest growth in the adult education field will occur in noneducational settings, particularly in private industry.

Although it is not possible to judge which forecast is most accurate, there are several identifiable variables which verify the notion that demand in general will increase. First, demographics provide clear evidence that the profile of the American population is changing. The average age of the population is steadily moving upward (in 1983 there were already more people over age sixty-five in America than there were teenagers). There will simply be more adults to serve in future years. In addition, the fastest growing segment of the American population are minority groups (twenty-five major cities already have minority majorities). These two realities lead to the conclusion that adult and continuing education will be the only real growth area in professional education (Hodgkinson, 1985).

The needs, values, and desires of this growing population of adults also need to be scrutinized. The passing of the baby boom generation, in particular, signals several new directions. It is apparent that those entering the work force are demanding more automony. Independence may become the most distinguishing factor of those who enter adulthood after the baby boomers (Deutsch, 1985). In addition, there is growing confusion about the value of education. In the past, completion of a bachelor's degree, a graduate degree, or a professional degree was deemed ample preparation for the work requirements of many adults. Perelman (1986) predicts that this trend already has changed. He identifies a growing number of MADMUPS (middle aged, downwardly mobile, unemployed professionals) who, despite higher levels of education, require constant retraining.

A growing number of adults and a changing set of needs, values, and desires suggest that program planning will become even more demanding than in the past. The process also must become more precise. For this reason, movement from technical models is viewed as an extremely high priority for adult education. Relevant planning is possible if it becomes individualized and input considerations become broader.

A NEW ERA OF ORGANIZATIONAL STUDY

In chapter 5 the three established eras of organizational study were reviewed. First, classical theory concentrated upon technical efficiency within the context of organizational automony. The second phase infused the consequences of internal social and political factors. The third era which emerged in the early 1960s focused upon the interdependence of the organization and its environment. Now a fourth stage of organizational study is emerging—the emphasis of social and cultural interdependence.

In part, these stages of organizational study have been generated by the proclivity of an increasing number of behavioral sciences to enter the arena of institutional studies. Sociologists, for instance, are the driving force of the emerging fourth era. Dissection of organizational life from a cultural perspective is based upon the premise that there exists both the technical and the social and cultural environments (Scott, 1983). The technical influence focuses upon factors such as specific demands for goods or services. The social and cultural encompasses normative behavior that emerges from linkages. A good example of environmental influences of normative behavior in educational organizations is the common perception of how teachers should behave: that is, teacher behavior is conditioned by societal views. These norms tend to penetrate organizational boundaries.

Exploration of cultural variables has enhanced the study of organizations. The potential value of this study to adult education programming is unlimited. Two perspectives are especially relevant. In the broader context of society, social and cultural analysis provides insights into the influence of values and norms on leadership behavior; that is, decisions and administrative behavior are influenced to some degree by nontechnical environmental pressures. Thus, the value of democratic decisions may supersede demands for expediency. The second perspective concentrates upon individual cultures. Each organization possesses myths, beliefs, values, and the like which influence behavior (Deal and Kennedy, 1982). For example, a company espousing the philosophy that "people always come first" may sacrifice profit to achieve customer satisfaction.

Each stage of organizational theory has expanded the opportunities for more effective leadership. The degree to which emerging information will enhance leadership behavior in the program planning process is yet to be determined. Although private and public organizations have been analyzed separately, scholars are just beginning to identify commonalities that permeate both. It is within this realm that the fourth stage of organizational theory offers promising insights to the program planner in adult education.

A NATIONAL PERSPECTIVE

America's departure from the notion that education is a youth activity is quite evident on the college campus. The profile of most student bodies is rapidly changing. Students now tend to be more heterogeneous with regard to age, and many universities are eager to serve the needs of those who are beyond the age of traditional undergraduate students (Fallon and Danglade, 1986). The philosophical importance of this trend lies not in the adjustments being made by the educational institutions (after all, many now welcome non-traditional students purely for economic reasons), but rather in the motives of the students. Adults are less apprehensive about attending organized educational programs. As a result, schools of the future, including elementary and secondary schools, will stay open longer and open their doors to different kinds of students—especially adults requiring training (Cetron, Soriano, and Gayle, 1985).

The acceptance of philosophical aspects of lifelong education can be attributed in large measure to economic and occupational realities. The average adult is apt to change jobs more frequently than his or her parents. Even for persons who maintain the same position throughout their work life, job requirements are less likely to remain stable. Naisbitt (1982) describes this trend:

> In education we are moving from the short-term considerations of completing our training at the end of high school or college to lifelong education and retraining. The whole idea of what education is will be reconceptualized during the next decade. (p. 93)

Thus, the realities of the world of work are contributing to changing attitudes about the value and utilization of education. Even though this is true, America continues to struggle with the issue of a national perspective for adult education.

The emphasis upon vocational and remedial programs has dominated adult education. This is most evident when one explores funding from federal sources. Merriam (1986) aptly explains one reason for a limited national perspective:

> To begin with, adult education's amorphous, diverse, albeit pervasive nature makes it difficult to grasp, to legislate for, to deal with in a comprehensive manner. Literacy and vocational training are relatively manageable concepts from which programs can be planned, implemented, and evaluated. (p. 5)

It is simplicity, once again, that indirectly retards the growth of adult education. A restricted perception of adult education creates tunnel vision. For instance, many organized learning experiences in noneducational environmen such as private corporations are not recognized as adult education. Classifi such endeavors as merely training encounters reduces consideration for ing theory, the needs of the learner, and the full potentialities of adul tion. In this manner, the failure to achieve a national perspective h negative implications for program planning.

If a new and more encompassing agenda can be implemented at federal and state levels, adult education is likely to emerge as a more sophisticated field of study and practice. In particular, programming could become a blend of considerations for the learner, the teaching act, the sponsoring organization, and society. By moving practice to this higher level, the values of a democratic society could be achieved and reinforced by lifelong education. To accomplish this goal, program development needs to be viewed as both an institutional process and as a teaching and learning process (Simpson, 1982).

MOVING FROM REACTIVE TO PROACTIVE

To a great extent, planning in education has been a reaction to existing conditions (Peterson, 1986): that is, most programs are developed out of necessity. Critical problems in private industry exemplify the manner in which adult education emerges as a reactive process. When conflict or similar dysfunctions occur, the organization as an entity strives to adjust. The development of adult education in most industrial sectors represents a reaction to unfavorable situations. Only in recent years have some enlightened corporations begun to explore the circuitous benefits that emerge for their organizations when educational programs are used to address the individual workers's needs and desires.

Another form of reaction can be observed in organizations when they develop programs simply because resources to do so are made available. For example, a school district may engage in adult basic education because the federal government makes millions of dollars available. Failure to pursue such revenues generates criticism. Citizens often expect local governmental agencies to obtain every dollar for services that is available. A reactive mode such as this reinforces the traditional path pursued by programmers—one based upon an internal perspective emphasizing the organization's needs, resources, capabilities, and limitations. This confined process for planning adult education ignores society and the learner (Sample and Kaufman, 1986).

Many scholars are arguing that the maturity of adult education as a force in society will be predicated upon a proactive stance toward programming (for example, Brookfield, 1986). In the absence of planning learning experiences designed to meet several critical needs simultaneously, adult education is likely to continue as a restricted asset. Imagine for a moment that federal, state, and local governments cooperatively determine that education is to be funded as lifelong process. Imagine that incentives are created for philosophical reasons rather than as reactions to problems. Such commitments to enhancing the ty of individual lives and the quality of society encourage proactive programming.

Most importantly, proactive planning allows adult education to become a vehicle for shaping the future. Too often, practitioners assume a fatalistic attitude about what lies ahead. They perceive their role as one of adjusting to crisis after crisis. As society becomes more reliant upon information and critical thinking skills, education is apt to become a more valued service. With complex and varied information at hand, most adults will find the use of information to be a higher priority than the generation of information. Proactive program planning permits the prevailing philosophy and values to influence directions in personal lives, corporate environments, and society. If and when this occurs, adult education will increase in stature. At this level of maturity, planning requires models that surpass the technical approaches of the past.

PROFESSIONAL EDUCATION OR HUMAN RESOURCES DEVELOPMENT

One burning debate within adult education today relates to the degree to which the preparation programs for practitioners should abandon an association with professional education (that is, the foundations of education) and move toward human resources development (that is, staff development and training). There is little doubt that private industry is rapidly becoming one of the largest providers of adult education. Furthermore, these organizations are likely to provide the most extrinsically rewarding environment for practitioners (higher salaries, better working conditions). Therefore, there is a growing interest in tailoring academic studies to those practitioners who intend to seek employment in business companies. This interest is intensified by the reality that a growing number of graduate students in adult education are already employed by commercial companies. These students are likely to be personnel managers, supervisors, or persons with business administration backgrounds aspiring to such positions.

Recent surveys of existing doctoral programs and of professors of adult education have provided insight into the division that exists with regard to the issue of professional education. Thirty percent of the doctoral programs in adult education in the United States require students to complete three or more courses in educational foundations (such as history of education or philosophy of education). Forty-three percent require two or less courses, and 27 percent require no work in educational foundations. When asked if requirements in educational foundations should be sustained, 12 percent of the professors strongly agreed, 43 percent agreed, 24 percent disagreed, and 6 percent strongly disagreed (Kowalski and Weaver, 1986). These results exemplify a difference of opinion that could have serious implications for the future of administration in adult education.

Assuming that programs do move toward human resources development, it is plausible that some degree and certification options will emerge outside of departments, schools, and colleges of education. For example, schools of business may decide that they ought to be preparing specialists in human resources development. Such decisions may not be objectionable if links between those who prepare educators and those who prepare managers can be established and maintained. But universities tend to be very bureaucratic entities in which the faculties of various divisions are protective of their domain. Galbraith and Murk (1986) argue that the foundational aspects of adult education make colleges of education the logical providers of such graduate programs. Pointing out the existing diversity of practice, they contend that locating academic programs in various departments and colleges would only add confusion to the mission of adult education.

The decision of whether to embrace a professional education identity is critical to the future of programming for at least two reasons. (1) A departure from the traditional position of professional education increases the likelihood that adult education will not remain the exclusive domain of departments, schools, and colleges of education. Under these conditions, programming may be taught in conjunction with existing planning courses in disciplines where learning theory and the like are not high priorities. For example, a business college may simply require students to take a standard planning course already offered for graduate students in management, marketing, or similar specializations. (2) The arguments regarding the philosophical and social issues of adult education come mainly from educational perspectives: that is, they originate outside the domain of organizational concerns. Since human resources development relates heavily to organizational development, it is apparent that diminishing requirements in educational foundations reduce the likelihood that factors such as values and social needs will be infused into program development.

Accordingly, the movement away from technical, linear models of planning seems to depend somewhat upon the direction the profession will take with regard to the issue of professional education versus human resources development. By studying sociology, philosophy, and similar foundations courses, students gain exposure to issues that assume special prominence in planning adult education. Where the line will be drawn between education and staff development will be an integral decision for all of adult education, but a particularly relevant one for program planning.

ADULT EDUCATION AS A FIELD OF STUDY

Closely related to the issue of professional education is the maturity of adult education as a field of study. Criticisms have become more frequent as adult education proliferates in practice. Plecas and Sork (1986) refer to the study of adult education as an "undisciplined discipline." They contend that two fundamental functions of a discipline are lacking—cumulative knowledge and theory building. Throughout this book, this point has been reinforced with special reference to program planning.

The status of organizing and planning adult education programs is an excellent example of the lack of maturity in graduate studies and in practice. Many of the models proposed are simply adaptations to linear, technical approaches used in business and industry. Even those that attempt to be more sophisticated tend to be adaptations from the business world (for example, Spikes and Spikes, 1986). As pointed out earlier in the book, Sork and Buskey (1986) examined program models in adult education and judged that these models (1) lacked cumulative knowledge and (2) failed to provide theoretical explanations.

Some may question why this text has devoted so much attention to organizational theory. The intent was to provide the reader with an understanding of how organizational climate can dictate individual behavior, even the behavior of a programmer in adult education. In the absence of this understanding, many practitioners are prone to accept the notion that organizational climate is determined solely by the adaptations to peremptory environmental forces (Hrebiniak and Joyce, 1985). This belief is the breeding ground for reactionary planning. On the other hand, there are those who myopically believe that organizational climate is simply a matter of choice, that management decisions determine whether an organization is open or closed. In reality, organizational behavior results from a mixture of choice and environmental adaptations (Hrebiniak and Joyce, 1985). This being the case, the practitioner must possess more than a proper philosophy. He or she also must depend upon the skills and insights related to organizational analysis. The infusion of organizational theory into planning models, especially the interactive models discussed in chapter 7, illustrates how cumulative knowledge and theoretical explanations can serve to improve adult education leadership.

The maturity of adult education becomes the critical factor determining the future paths of program planning. If research and resulting theory continue to become more prominent, improvements can be expected in academic studies initially, and in practice ultimately. As Boone (1985) suggests, the answer for improving programming lies not in recruiting specialists from other fields, but rather in improving the abilities of generalists within the field. Failure to mature may cause adult education to retreat to a position of preparing teachers for basic programs, and the leaders and programmers will be produced by other entities in higher education and in the business world.

SUMMARY

Those studying to be administrators of adult education today must be prepared to deal with a most uncertain future. For this reason, projecting tomorrow's needs is a critical aspect of program planning. The value of this activity lies not so much in the ability to cope, but rather in the ability to direct. Understanding the issues which will affect the future makes it more likely that practitioners can determine future directions.

This chapter addressed four issues which are likely to affect the organization and planning of adult education. They include developing a national perspective, moving to a proactive stance in planning, maintaining an identity as a part of professional education, and adult education reaching maturity as a field of study. The directions of these issues will shape the challenges and activities of planners in the next twenty-five years.

FOR FURTHER DISCUSSION

1. List the ways that a national perspective could influence program planning.

2. Is it likely that schools of business will attempt to offer degrees in adult education? Defend your response.

3. Describe theoretical explanations. What relationship does research have to theoretical explanations?

4. Take a position for or against the movement toward human resources development in adult education. What are the likely consequences for program planning?

5. If organizational behavior is indeed a mixture of adaptations of the organization to its environment and philosophical choices by the leadership of the organization, list the ways a programmer may be influenced by both factors.

REFERENCES

Boone, E. (1985). *Developing programs in adult education.* Englewood Cliffs, NJ: Prentice-Hall.

Brookfield, S. (1986). *Understanding and facilitating adult learning.* San Francisco: Jossey-Bass.

Cetron, M., Soriano, B. and Gayle, M. (1985). Schools of the future. *Futurist, 19*(4), 18–23.

Deal, T., and Kennedy, A. (1982). *Corporate cultures.* Reading, MA: Addison-Wesley.

Deutsch, R. (1985). Tomorrow's work force: New values in the workplace. *Futurist, 19*(6), 8–11.

Fallon, J., and Danglade, J. (1986). The future of higher education in relation to adult education. *Eastern Education Journal, 18*(2), 20–24.

Galbraith, M., and Murk, P. (1986). Adult education ought to be the exclusive domain of colleges of education. *Eastern Education Journal, 18*(2), 13–17.

Hoare, C. (1982). Future issues in adult education: A review of the literature of the seventies. *Adult Education, 33*(1), 55–69.

Hodgkinson, H. (1985). *All one system: Demographics of education, kindergarten through graduate school.* Washington, D. C.: Institute for Educational Leadership.

Hrebiniak, L., and Joyce, W. (1985). Organizational adaptation: Strategic choice of environmental determinism. *Administrative Science Quarterly, 30,* 336–349.

Kowalski, T., and Weaver, R. (1986). Graduate studies in adult education: An analysis of doctoral programs and professorial opinions. *Proceedings, 1986 midwest research-to-practice conference in adult, community, and continuing education.* Muncie, IN: Ball State University.

Merriam, S. (1986). Developing a national perspective. *Eastern Education Journal, 18*(2), 4–8.

Naisbitt, J. (1982). *Megatrends.* New York: Warner Books.

Perelman, L. (1986). Learning our lesson: Why school is out. *Futurist, 20*(2), 13–16.

Peterson, M. (1986). Continuity, challenge and change: An organizational perspective on planning past and future. *Planning in Higher Education, 14*(3), 6–15.

Plecas, D., and Sork, T. (1986). Adult education: Curing the ills of an undisciplined discipline. *Adult Education Quarterly, 37,* 48–62.

Sample, J., and Kaufman, R. (1986). A holistic program development model for adult educators (part one). *Lifelong Learning, 9*(4), 18–23.

Scott, W. (1983). The organization of environments: Network, cultural, and historical elements. In J. Meyer and W. Scott (Eds.), *Organizational environments (pp. 155–178).* Beverly Hills, CA: Sage Publications.

Simpson, E. (1982). Program development: A model. In C. Kelvins (Ed.), *Materials and methods in adult and continuing education* (pp. 92–98). Los Angeles: Klevens Publications.

Sork, T. & Buskey, J. (1986). A descriptive and evaluative analysis of program planning literature, 1950–1983. *Adult Education Quarterly, 36*(2), 86–96.

Spikes, W. & Spikes, J. (1986). An educator's guide to strategic planning. *Lifelong Learning, 9*(7), 6–11.

Author Index

Subject Index